MW00668257

THE
FOUNDATION
OF A
SUCCESSFUL
LIFE

BY JOE FLORENTINE AND ERICA FLORENTINE

Want to see your life change for the better right before your eyes? It's as simple as learning and practicing the lessons in *The Foundation of a Successful Life*. We all want something out of life, whether it's a personal goal, a professional goal, an academic goal or a combination of these. This book offers a tried and true formula for turning those goals into reality. The sooner you begin to implement these lessons, the sooner you'll begin seeing results!

The Foundation of a Successful Life will walk you through proven steps to success, like understanding what makes *you* happy, creating a positive mindset, goal setting, planning, turning hurdles into advantages and much more. These lessons have been used for generations by the world's most successful people to get anything they wanted out of life… and now you, too, can follow suit.

It does not matter where you are in life right now. All that matters is where you want to go from this point forward. Picking up this book is the first step toward finding happiness and success in your life, however it is that you personally define happiness and success. The time is *now*. Are you ready?

The Foundation of a Successful Life
© 2020 by Success Cornerstone LLC

ISBN: 978-1-73456-211-8

To our family and friends, thank you for supporting us through this project! We couldn't have done it without you. Specifically, we'd like to dedicate this book to Diane Florentine – mother to Joe and nana to Erica – who led her life putting everyone ahead of herself. Upon her passing, she inspired us to write this book as a means of being of service to all, just as she was.

TABLE OF CONTENTS

FOREWORD

My career in real estate was built from the ground up.

I grew up in a small town in New Jersey with three brothers and three sisters. My dad worked hard to keep food on the table while my mom worked hard to keep our house feeling like a home.

I went through high school as a below-average student and was barely accepted into my local community college. Two days into the first semester, I walked out. I knew this wouldn't go over well with my dad, so I needed a plan, and I needed one quick. After scanning the newspaper's Help Wanted section, one ad jumped out: "Earn big money in Real Estate!" I called immediately.

They said they'd hire me as soon as I had my real estate license, which would require some schooling. I said I was in, without a doubt.

So, for the next few months, I studied to get my license during the day and worked the midnight shift at an aluminum factory to keep cash in my pocket. Once my license was secured, I was hired by the real estate agency, as promised, and I started brokering, buying and selling homes for them. Things seemed to be progressing in the right direction.

The plan took a detour, however, when my dad's company announced it was being sold. About to be out of a job and with a family to support, he decided to start a lunch truck business. He would need my brother Bob and I—his two eldest children, just 18 and 19 years old at the time—to help him with it… 1,300 miles away from home.

We dropped everything—including my new real estate career—and made the move to Florida. Despite the hurdle, I knew I'd eventually get my plan back on track, and I was right. About six months later, I was able to move back to New Jersey and pick up where I left off. I continued to work hard to build my career in residential real estate and, after some time, was making great money.

The money coming in continued to grow and grow over the next couple of decades… until it quickly stopped in its tracks. Then, it disappeared completely.

See, when the real estate market crashed in 2008, I lost everything and more. **In fact, in the fall of 2009, my net worth was negative $120,000.**

I was living in a home I could no longer afford with my wife and middle-school-aged daughter. My other two children were away at college, so bills were piling up from every angle—and I had absolutely zero income. At this point it seemed the harder I was working, the less money I was making.

It could've been viewed as a tough time to say the least. There were many days I'd wake up wondering if this situation was going to get the best of me… but it didn't. Why? I never let it.

My mind had been trained through decades of practice under a range of self-help coaches to find the positive in every situation and expect good outcomes no matter what. Some days it proved easier than others, but I worked at it regularly, always showing gratitude and positivity every chance I could. For example, as soon as things initially took a turn for the worse, I started a gratitude journal that I wrote in for 5–10 minutes every single day. I'd write things like, "I am grateful for my wife. She is really my best friend and I love spending time with her." I'd revisit these entries whenever I felt a negative thought trying to creep in. The entries always helped to turn my mind in a positive direction and get me feeling good. Despite my dire financial standing at the time, I was aware I had many blessings in my life and the gratitude journal served as a constant reminder of that. The odds may have appeared to be against me from an outsider's perspective, but I refused to believe it.

I was first exposed to the teachings of the self-help author Dr. Napoleon Hill through his world-famous book, *Think & Grow Rich*, when I was just 20 years old. I studied and applied his teachings from that point forward—and those teachings never failed in helping me succeed. In my adult years, I was exposed to countless other self-help experts and what I found is this: While each of these experts approached the topic from a slightly different angle, they all had the same underlying message in common—with a positive mindset, an expectation of great outcomes and a willingness to take action, you will always hold the key to living a happy and successful life. (In fact, the teachings of Dr. Hill and others inspired me so much that I recently became a certified course instructor for The Napoleon Hill Foundation. Some lessons that we'll discuss throughout this book will build on the topics I teach in the course and that people have been using for generations to find happiness and success in their lives. You can learn more about the work of The Napoleon Hill Foundation by visiting www.naphill.org.)

With these self-help lessons in mind, when things went downhill financially for me in 2009, I did everything in my power to stay both happy and positive and to bring myself back to financial success. To initially stay afloat, I started auctioning homes for a small commission as an immediate step. However, I was honest with myself that this tactic would never manage to fully get me back on my feet. I knew there was something bigger and better that was about to work out for me if I kept an eye out for it—I could *feel* it.

I set a specific goal and elected to make it a big one—to free myself of debt and to acquire a net worth of over $10,000,000 by December 31, 2015. With my goal in place, a positive mindset, and the confidence and will to win, I needed to put a plan into action.

A couple of nights later, my wife, Fran, suggested we buy a rental property, moving away from what we'd previously been doing with residential real estate. This way, she said, we would always have income even during bad real estate cycles. We had been in residential real estate for many years with great success during good times but many difficulties during the bad times. We knew from experience that the smaller residential properties did not always work well for good cash flow, but we'd seen people with larger rental apartments and commercial properties do very well.

The more I thought about Fran's suggestion, the more I liked it and the more I could visualize my goal coming true. This, I thought, could be my chance to turn the adversity of the collapsed real estate market into a benefit for myself and my family.

Fran and I decided to look into the worst real estate markets in the United States and try to buy an apartment complex there in order to get the best possible deal. We did some research and one jumped off the page... Fort Myers, Florida. We didn't know anything about the area, but the one thing I knew from years of studying successful people was that it was the winter home of two of my favorites: Thomas Edison and Henry Ford. This was where my goal was bound to be achieved—no doubt!

We made appointments to see several properties there and booked the next flight out. I remember being overcome with optimism as Fran and I were sitting in the airport on our way there.

"This is really going to happen," I said to Fran. "I can feel it." You know that feeling, when you just *know* something is right and that things are about to come together for you?

After seeing the properties and making some offers, ultimately an offer was accepted on one of the apartment buildings. We were able to get the money together to purchase it through a mortgage and a handful of private investors. In less than 18 months, we were able to turn the project around and almost double the value of the property.

Due to the amount of money our investors made from that initial project, they wanted to continue to invest in new projects. They spread the word about the amount of money they were making to other people they knew, so our list of investors continued to grow with each successful project. Even better, each of those investors continued to want to invest larger amounts of money. Within six years of that first deal, we had over $60,000,000 in income-producing real estate assets.

And, it all began with the right mindset, a goal, and the purchase of that very first apartment complex—something I would have never purchased had the real estate market not crashed. This further solidified for me the fact that there is—without a doubt—a benefit to be had in every adversity. The real estate market crash pushed me to much bigger real estate projects and allowed my business to flourish, forever changing my life. Having met and exceeded my goal, I have now retired from the real estate business and collect residual rental income each month.

It was fulfilling to achieve my goal, and while not all people equate success with money, I will say that the biggest benefit I've found in acquiring money is the freedom it provides. It's offered me the freedom to travel, take time off to spend with my family and friends, give back to those in need, and—importantly—the freedom to take time to write this book, which I hope will help people in achieving happiness and success in their lives. This book is not just about finding professional and financial success. It is about finding success in any way *you* define the term. It's applicable to all areas of life—and I hope you find the lessons to be as useful as I have.

Nothing you will find in this book is based on theory. It is based on the exact model I, and countless others throughout history, have followed in order to live a more successful life.

I recount my personal real estate story to assure you that you can *always* find success in your life no matter the circumstances you're up against. While each of us will define success differently, with the right habits in place, you can attain whatever it is you want in life, whether success for you translates to something professional, personal, academic or a combination of them.

Practicing the lessons found in this book has helped me to live my best life possible. I've had great relationships with my parents (God rest their souls), my wonderful wife, Fran, of 35 years, and my three children—Erica, who wrote this book with me; Joey, who has taken over our real estate business; and Lia, who recently graduated college and has just entered the workforce. I've also maintained thriving relationships with my brothers and sisters, in laws, friends and business associates. As I've mentioned, living a successful life is not just about money (and for some it's not about money at all). It's about achieving whatever it is that brings *you* happiness. For me, that has been a combination of achieving my professional goals and maintaining excellent relationships with my loved ones. I owe all my success to the lessons in this book. I hope you find them just as useful as I have.

Enjoy this book and use it to achieve whatever it is you want. As you begin applying the lessons, watch and see how your life quickly begins to go in any direction you desire.

Best of luck to you in your journey to living a more successful life!

Joe Florentine
Author of The Foundation of a Successful Life
Co-Founder/CEO of Success Cornerstone

INTRODUCTION

This may be the most important book you read in your lifetime. If you learn and apply the lessons we discuss here it will serve as an entryway for you to a new world of life-changing success and happiness.

This book, *The Foundation of a Successful Life*, is designed to help you become more successful in your life in every regard. It is designed to teach you how to think, persist, solve problems and win in your personal life, your professional life, your academic life or a combination of them. Here we will encourage you to go after whatever it is you want in life... and get it!

This is the foundation of a proven success philosophy whose origins are based on research on—and interviews with—hundreds of the most successful people in the world over the past 100 years. Both of us as authors have successfully applied these principles in our own lives as well, in addition to observing how others we know first-hand have used and benefitted from them.

You will notice throughout the book we use the word "we" when speaking to you. "We" is intended to represent both authors—past and present experts in the field of self-help and researchers of the habits of successful and happy people. Think of it as a collective group speaking directly to you and passing along the knowledge we've acquired to help you lead a more successful life in all areas.

In this book, you will learn how to turn your goals into reality through proven steps that will stay with you for the rest of your life. We hope you enjoy *The Foundation of a Successful Life* and that you begin to utilize these lessons as soon as possible. Do not be surprised if you begin to see immediate results once you do.

Most people have never been introduced or exposed to a philosophy of success, let alone a proven philosophy. This book has been developed through actual application of success principles and techniques learned, studied and applied from some of the greatest self-help authors in history including Dr. Napoleon Hill, Tony Robbins, Abraham-Ester Hicks, Earl Nightingale, W. Clement Stone, Rhonda Byrne, Og Mandino, Jack Canfield and more. We have now brought the basis of some of their teachings and more into several simple, modern-day lessons that will teach you how to live a more successful life—no matter how you define success.

Again, this is a proven philosophy, not just a theory, and we say that with complete confidence. Not only have we as authors successfully applied these lessons, but some of its basis is in the teachings of some of the greatest self-help authors of all time, including Dr. Hill, who we (and many others) consider the Godfather of self-help. He spent over 20 years interviewing and following over 500 of the most successful people in the United States to determine what it was they had done that most people had not.

This is your opportunity to now find your own similar success using modern-age lessons.

How does this book differ from reading any other book in this genre? This book is unique in that it includes ideas and proven lessons from a wide range of viewpoints on the topic of finding happiness and success. We've spent years combing through research, books and courses in order to bring you the best, most effective information there is on the topic. And, we've laid it out in an easily digestible manner so that you can follow the process step-by-step without feeling overwhelmed. What's more, we have personally used these lessons in our lives to achieve what we want—so we know, with complete certainty, that when practiced consistently these lessons can help you to do the very same.

It doesn't matter where you are in life right now, what matters is where you are going, from this moment forward. When you are done with this book you will no longer find yourself making excuses and protesting that you don't have the same opportunities or advantages that others have. As you will see, many successes were achieved by those with very lowly beginnings and those who faced poverty, lack of education, physical handicaps, and more. These individuals all managed to rise above their circumstances to achieve great success.

It does not matter how old you are right now as you're picking up this book. Maybe you're a teenager who is still in high school and just starting out in life, or perhaps you're in your later years and itching to find success. Great success can be achieved *at any age*. Consider Colonel Sanders, founder of Kentucky Fried Chicken, who did not find success in his career until after the age of 60.[1] At the time he had been running a restaurant for several years before deciding to retire and bring his chicken recipe on the road. With a goal to promote his chicken recipe, Colonel Sanders went from restaurant to restaurant with a persistent attitude, often cooking his fried chicken recipe on the spot for restaurant owners. After much time and hard work, he had hundreds of franchises selling his trademark recipe. He went from practically $0 net worth to millions, all in the later years of his life.

This book will cover a broad scope of lessons that will lead you to live a more successful life overall.

If you are reading this book in conjunction with our Action Steps Manual, we couldn't be more excited for you and wish you much luck with it. Those who would like to purchase our Action Steps Manual who haven't already done so can do so now by visiting www.SuccessCornerstone.com. The Action Steps Manual provides you with weekly action steps for each lesson taught in this book and is sure to move you toward what you want in life more expeditiously. Top success and self-help coaches we are familiar with recommend investing between 5 percent and 10 percent of a person's yearly income in themselves—either through taking courses, reading books, attending seminars or the like. If you're looking for a guided deep-dive into the lessons within this book, our Action Steps Manual might be the best bet for you to invest in.

If you're reading this book on your own and not paced out with our Action Steps Manual, we encourage you to move slowly through the chapters. There is a lot of information here and many exercises we encourage you to practice. Our recommendation, based on what we've seen work best for readers, is to master one lesson (or one chapter) per week over a 20-week period. This pace will be beneficial to you in fully absorbing the lessons. If 20 weeks seems like a very long time, think of it this way—20 weeks is relatively short considering this foundation will be carried through your entire lifetime! Take your time to perfect these lessons. Practice, practice, and practice again.

While reading this book you will discover the lessons within can be applied to anything you desire in life, whether that's money, better health, better friendships, better relationships, a substantially happier life and or whatever else. You will find a more successful life overall. Success is what you want, what you define as success and what is going to make you happy.

You will find this book makes no reference to any religion and does not contain any religious overtones. This leaves you to your own beliefs on that very important subject. Powers greater than yourself are simply referred to on occasion as Forces of Nature. Keep in mind that your own personal beliefs may certainly be substituted for these references throughout the book.

It is our sincere desire that the lessons described in this book will soon be taught in the public school system, producing a new generation of positive thinkers who go through life with the ongoing intention to not only benefit themselves, but everyone associated with them and society in general.

We will admit that this book is not for everyone. If you do not truly desire success in life and are content leading a "normal life," that is fine and we wish you all the best. But, *and this is a big but*, if you desire to achieve more out of life and are willing to follow a proven blueprint to accomplish that, this book is for you.

Before you lies the opportunity to begin a life of success and happiness. We sincerely hope you will take advantage of this opportunity and do something with this book that will not only improve your life, but the lives of future generations to come.

We suggest two very important points before you start:

1. **If you doubt even for a moment that what you are learning in this book is true, we strongly encourage you to reach out to the most successful person who you know.**

   When you reach out, share what you are learning with them and ask them if it's true. Not only will they say yes, but likely they will add more to it by elaborating on their path to success and their personal thoughts on the topic. You will find that some may practice these principles consciously, while others may do them unconsciously, but nevertheless they utilize the lessons in this book one way or the other. Likely, they will encourage you to do the same. They may even take a long-term interest in you, how you're doing with the book and your path to success.

2. **Do not let others discourage you.**

   We call those people "dream stealers." Most of the time they are the people closest to you, (e.g., parents, siblings, romantic partners, best friends, and so on). They don't mean any harm to you and believe they are looking out for your best interests, however, perhaps they have never read what you're reading and never practiced anything you are about to learn. Their intentions may be good; however, they may not understand what you're learning and have their own predetermined ideas about success, happiness and life in general.

Your first real test will be overcoming the dream stealers. Are you going to allow the opinion of others to sway how you are going to live your life, or are you going to think for yourself? Consider this important point: If you want an opinion about something, ask the right person. For example, if you want to know how to make more money, ask someone who has it, not someone who doesn't. If you want advice on relationships, ask someone who has been successful in relationships, not someone who has had failing relationships. If you want advice on health, ask someone who is healthy and strong, not someone who is always sick and tired. Seek advice from people who are qualified to give it, not just anyone.

The opportunity to live a more successful life begins now. It's up to *you* to decide what you are going to do with it. We are about to lay out the foundation of success for you and we hope you seize it! We look forward to you joining the ranks of the self-thinkers and achievers in life. Have fun and enjoy the process!

CHAPTER 1

What Makes *You* Happy?

H ow do you define the word happiness? According to Merriam-Webster, happiness is defined as a state of well-being and content-ment.[2] But what makes *you* feel content? What does happiness mean to you, personally?

Chances are your answer will be slightly different from other people you know. For some people, happiness is most easily felt when spending time with friends and family. For others, happiness is most easily felt when a big achievement is made at work or a monetary goal has been reached. Some feel happy when they're shopping, or exercising, or painting, or getting a spa service. Maybe your answer is a combination of all of these things and more.

It's important to understand what it is that makes you feel happy in order to live a more successful life. Many people find it difficult to understand success because they don't know what it is that makes them feel good. They're conditioned to immediately associate success with professional achievements, but that is not what this is all about.

Because these individuals never take the time to understand what makes them happy, many of them find themselves stuck in a job they don't partic-ularly enjoy, for instance, and they float through life feeling mediocre every day. Ultimately, they may feel as though they've never really accomplished anything of meaning to them.

Happiness and living a successful life both go hand-in-hand. Happiness and success are each very personal things and their definitions both vary from person to person. What makes one person feel happy might be something that makes another person feel unhappy. What translates to success for one person might not translate to anything at all to another person. To understand what you're specifically working toward achieving in life—and how to remain happy along the way to achieving it—you must come to terms with what it is that makes you feel good.

> *"The most important thing is to enjoy your life—to be happy—it's all that matters."*
> *—Audrey Hepburn*[3]

Before we do any self-examination, consider the fact that many people let others influence their own definition of happiness. Think of this example: A recent college graduate was encouraged by his parents to attend a particular university and choose finance as a major. Now heading into his first year as a financial advisor, his parents are thrilled, as the company he's landed a job at is starting him with a six-figure salary—more than the parents make collectively. It all seems amazing, right? But what if this recent college graduate hates working with numbers? What if, all along, he's found finance to be an intolerable job field and only followed this path because he was encouraged to by his parents? What if what he really wants to do is be a history teacher, let's say?

There are endless outside influences in your life that will try to guide you on a certain path based on how they view happiness. In the previous example, perhaps the parents' definition of happiness is being able to live in monetary abundance and they believed their son should feel the same way. This has, in turn, led their son on the wrong path in terms of what happiness means to him. He isn't doing what truly makes him happy—he's doing what he believes *should* make him happy.

Parents are strong influences, but so are friends, coworkers, neighbors, acquaintances, television personalities, social media influencers, and so many more. We're constantly being told what happiness and success means from other people. If we don't take the time to fully consider what it truly means to us, we can spend our entire lives on the wrong path.

Now, let's consider another example: A young woman and her husband recently welcomed their second child. She is a stay-at-home mom and she and her family live a comfortable life in a small town. Her relatives all live within a few-mile radius of her which she loves. For this young mother, this translates to happiness. Her success was achieved in life by having a family and getting to spend as much of her time with her kids and family as possible. Might her goals change in the future? Sure thing. But for now, she is as happy as could be.

However, her female friends have all made their careers their #1 priority. For them, success and happiness are attained at this point in their lives through work, and work alone. They often give their friend a hard time about why she isn't working and ask her if she's fulfilled without having a job. It leaves the young mother questioning her judgement. But she shouldn't! Her definition of happiness is different than her friends' definition—and that is OK.

In all cases, we should never feel we need to question the things that make us feel happy because of what others say. It is *your life,* and only you can determine what will make you happy.

You'll hear this time and time again as you're reading this book, but a major piece of advice we can give you in order to live a more successful life is this: Stop concerning yourself with what other people are doing and saying. Their goals are different from yours. Their happiness is defined differently than yours. To live the most successful life possible, you need to focus on *you!*

You see, success—at its core—is driven by happiness. You can be worth a billion dollars, but if you're working around the clock and never getting to spend time with your family, maybe you're not happy after all. We wouldn't consider this living a successful life, because from our point of view living a *successful* life is living a *happy* life as well.

Now let's dive into what makes you happy. Take a quick break from reading, grab a piece of paper and a pencil, and we want you to write down a list of all of the people, places, things, and activities that make you feel happy. Again, don't be influenced by others. This is all about you.

Once your list is complete, take a long, hard look at it. Visualize each item on the list and think of how you feel when you're experiencing each of them. Let that feeling take over. It's possible you'll find a smile coming to your face as you're doing this. The things that make you happy will also make you *feel good.*

How you feel about the thought you're thinking tells you if you're heading in the right direction for what you want in life. Read that last sentence again. Then, read it again.

Keep this "happiness list" on hand and come back to it often. Add to it and/or subtract from it as needed. As you go through different stages of your life, don't be surprised when there are some changes to what it is that makes you happy.

When revisiting your list, not only should you review it as we just did, but you should act on it when possible too. Naturally some items will be easier to act on than others, but that doesn't mean you can't begin to plan ahead on some of the bigger items. Is Paris on the list of places that make you feel happy? We're not expecting you to visit Paris every week, but perhaps right now you can start planning a trip there for next year. Even that planning process will bring you happiness because you will find yourself envisioning what it's like to be there.

Why is it so important to create and keep your happiness list on hand? Because, contrary to popular belief, **happiness is something that should be experienced along a person's path to success, not just once they've achieved a given goal.**

This is where a lot of people get it wrong.

How many times have you heard someone say, "I'll be happy when…" followed by a goal they want to achieve? It's commonplace for people to think happiness and success work like this. But they don't! Is every minute that you're working toward a goal going to feel wonderful? Of course not. But there are certainly going to be many great moments along the path, without a doubt. The trick is knowing and understanding the things that make you happy (see: your happiness list) and allowing yourself to experience them as often as possible throughout your life.

If you're someone who is living with the "I'll be happy when…" mentality, living a successful life is going to be very challenging for you. This is because, likely, once you've achieved a given goal, there is going to be something else you want to achieve next, and something after that, and something else after that. With the "I'll be happy when…" mentality, when will you ever allow yourself to finally be happy?

Consider the example of J.K. Rowling. Now she's an internationally known name and worth an estimated $1 billion, but it was not an easy journey to the top for J.K. Rowling to say the least. J.K. Rowling has said that at a certain point prior to finding success from writing the Harry Potter book series, she was jobless, a single parent and "as poor as it is possible to be in modern Britain, without being homeless." Even after coming up with the concept for the *first Harry Potter book, she continued to face hurdle after hurdle in her path to completing it—from the death of her mother to a severe case of depression.*

However, she always found happiness in writing, so that is where she continued to stay focused. Following a passion in life that made her feel happy gave her the ongoing drive to overcome anything she was going through, including initial publisher rejections of her first book. Ultimately, by following her own personal happiness, she found success beyond measure.[4]

In the case where today marks Day 1 of your path to success,—even though you may be seemingly many miles away from achieving a goal that you may have in mind—we guarantee there is something for you to be happy about *today.* Just look at that happiness list again. It's there, we assure you.

Let us say this here and now—you have one shot at life. One single attempt to make the most of it. Do you want to live it being happy, or do you want to live it *waiting* to be happy? We'll let you decide.

"Folks are usually about as happy as they make their minds up to be."
—Abraham Lincoln[5]

If you've decided that you want to live your life being happy, keep this sentence in your back pocket and repeat it as often as you can: *I am happy and I expect great things to happen to me.*

In an upcoming chapter we'll get into further detail on creating a positive mindset in order to achieve anything you want in life, but for now we'll just say that our minds are an incredibly powerful tool. No outside force, either positive or negative, can affect you if you do not allow it to do so.

That tough circumstance you may be facing right now—it won't have the power to keep you in an unhappy state if your mind does not allow it to. You, and only you, are in complete control of how you mentally view and react to everything in your life.

> *"It isn't what you have or who you are or where you are or what you are doing that makes you happy or unhappy. It is what you think about it."*
> *—Dale Carnegie*[6]

You can *have* anything you want. You can *achieve* anything you want. You can *be* anything you want. All you have to do is decide it to be so.

So what if you're not there just yet? Maybe the reason you picked up this book is because you're in a rut. You have things you want to achieve in life but you feel like you're constantly being pushed down. You may constantly find yourself wondering why others around you can get want they want but you can't. Stop here. A lot of times people who are in a rut in terms of happiness and achieving their goals are simultaneously feeling like it's unfair that it comes to others easier than it comes to them. If this seems relatable, that could be the very thing dragging you down! You can have everything they have as well, but you need to figure out what your own happiness means and choose to be positive as a very first step.

Let's consider some characteristics that might be holding people back from being happy:

- Their current financial situation is lacking.
- They're prone to complaining.
- They're stuck in the past and can't seem to move forward from past mistakes.
- Their self-confidence is lacking.
- They're prone to feelings of jealousy.

- They've allowed a negative circumstance they were born into, or a current negative circumstance, to dictate their future.

All of these, and more, can be considered negative. Let's focus in on the last one for a moment. Have you ever said a statement like this one: "That person can achieve whatever they want in life, but for me it's impossible because of my circumstances"?

Your current circumstance does not define you, no matter what it is. It is not an indicator of how happy you'll be tomorrow and into the future. It does not prevent you from achieving anything you want. All your current circumstance defines is where you're at this very moment in time. Most any circumstance can be left behind *just like that,* as long as you decide to do so.

If any of the previously mentioned characteristics seem familiar to you it's time to move on from them. All of them will hold you back.

Instead of saying "I don't want my circumstances to remain as they are," say, "I am going to change my circumstances so that I can achieve everything I want."

Let go of the past. This is time for a fresh start. And, it's going to be amazing and filled with happiness, as long as you understand what happiness means to you and believe you will be happy.

You'll learn many times throughout this book that *like attracts like.* If you're thinking of positive things that make you feel happy, you will attract those things into your life. However, the opposite is true as well. If you're lacking in money, for example, you may feel unhappy and stressed constantly. In turn, your thoughts of lack of money are attracting more debt and financial problems. This is not a theory—this is fact. We will dive deeper into this in future chapters.

Whatever you believe, whether positive or negative, will be true *every single time.*

Focus on what it is that makes you happy instead of what it is that makes you unhappy.

Start to move away from things and people that don't make you happy and start spending more time with things and people that do make you happy. The whole point of living a more successful life is for you to feel good. Imagine yourself in the state of having already acquired that feeling of happiness. Imagine, too, what it feels like to have achieved success in the way you want it.

Begin to expect good things to happen to you. We'll help you to train your mind to do so, but for now, every time something that seems surprisingly good happens to you, your mind should immediately think, "Well, of course it did. I attracted that with my new positive mindset!"

Let's be completely honest: You're not going to feel happy at every single moment of every single day. The trick is that if you feel unhappiness creeping in, don't dwell on it. Spend less of your mental space on those things that make you unhappy compared to the things that make you happy. And, remember, only you can tell if what you're doing feels good or not.

Soon we'll talk at length about pinpointing a goal for yourself and your plan to achieve it. But, let us quickly say here that—just as your definition of happiness is different from others around you—your goal will likely be different as well. Some people reading this book perhaps want to start their own business, so their goal will be very professional. Others may have a far more personal goal, such as to find a spouse and start a family. Still, other readers who are at an earlier stage of their life may be focused solely on achieving success in school and getting into the right college. Goals can be whatever you want them to be. It must make sense to you and make you happy. Remember, your real goal in life is to be happy!

"There are no happier people on this planet than those who decide that they want something, define what they want, get

hold of the feeling of it even before it's manifestation and then joyously watch the unfolding as, piece by piece by piece, it begins to unfold. That's the feeling of your hands in the clay."

—Ester Hicks[7]

Achieving one's goal doesn't always have to equate to making money, or running a marathon, or winning a baking competition, though it can be one or all of those. No one has that answer except for you. And you should allow yourself to constantly feel happy along the path to achieving whatever it is you want to achieve. Only then will you be able to live a truly successful life.

CHAPTER 2

Uncovering and Changing Your Limiting Beliefs

All of us have beliefs when it comes to topics such as money and relationships. Some of our beliefs are apparent to us in our conscious mind. For instance, you may consciously consider how you feel right now about the topic of money and come to a quick and clear conclusion about your beliefs on the topic, the concept of you having money in excess, the concept of others having it in excess, and so on.

We all also have beliefs in our subconscious mind as well which can be less apparent. From a relationship perspective, maybe a person was raised by two parents who were divorced. Due to their divorce, the parents constantly told their child that relationships are all destined to fail. Maybe this person doesn't consciously realize it, but this could have seeped into their subconscious mind as a child and resulted in a poor belief about relationships as an adult, and likely, poor outcomes. Their mind has essentially been trained to believe all relationships will fail, so in turn, they find themselves in failing relationships.

Whether established in the conscious mind or subconscious mind, any belief that holds you back from achieving or attaining what you want in life can be considered a limiting belief. A limiting belief *limits* a person's ability to move forward and get the things they so desire. A limiting belief, whether it's rooted consciously or subconsciously, needs to be cleansed out of the mind and a new, positive belief needs to replace it.

"You begin to fly when you let go of self-limiting beliefs and allow your mind and aspirations to rise to greater heights."
—Brian Tracy[8]

Are there limiting beliefs that may be holding you back from achieving happiness and success in your life? Let's spend some time examining this.

At this point, you may not even be sure of what it is that's holding you back. Maybe there isn't anything, in which case that's wonderful! A quick way to figure out if there may be a limiting belief in play is to ask yourself this: Is there something you have been trying very hard to achieve or attain—whether personally, professionally or academically—but you just can't seem to make it happen? If so, chances are very good that at the core of what's holding you back is a limiting belief that needs to be changed.

Let's focus on money and relationships as two big areas where people tend to have limiting beliefs. Keep in mind that, should you uncover a limiting belief in other areas besides money and relationships, the techniques we discuss here to overcome the limiting belief can be applied to any area of your life.

We'll start with money. Through one's own thoughts, or through social heredity (the people around them), many people come to believe that money is the root of all evil. This notion is not only untrue, it is often initiated by those who *do not* have money. Often, people come to believe it is honorable to not have money and that anyone who has it must have done something wrong or is simply a bad person in general. As an example, a person who was born into a family who constantly struggled with money may come to feel they should remain in the same financial status as their parents and those around them who grew up similarly. In fact, this person may feel a sense of guilt even at the thought of having more money than others and at the thought of exceeding what they were taught to be the "financial norm." Over time, this person may mentally begin to believe they don't deserve financial success and they, in turn, spend their life barely getting by financially because they believe that is the expectation of them. Ultimately, those they encounter who *do* have money become thought of as an enemy.

This type of limiting belief about money will hold a person back from ever achieving great financial success, even if financial success is their goal in life and they put all their time and energy into achieving it. It's plain and simple: If you aspire to have financial success, it is imperative that you change any limiting belief about money from one of lack or struggle, to one of abundance and prosperity. You *must* have a positive belief about money to attain an abundant amount of money.

> *"If you accept a limiting belief, then it will become a truth for you."*
> —*Louise Hay*[8]

Starting to see how powerful the mind is? Your mind can *literally* hold you back from getting what you want if it's not working in your favor.

We're going to talk a lot throughout this book about the power of one's mind and the importance of remaining positive in order to get positive results. In a scenario where you may have a limiting belief as mentioned regarding money, you must use your mind to begin erasing it and replacing it with a positive viewpoint. You need to start believing that you have the right to be financially successful. Every time a negative thought about money crosses your mind, counter it with a positive thought.

The same thing can be applied to relationships, be it romantic relationships or relationships with friends, coworkers and the like. A common limiting belief about romantic relationships, for example, is that there is no way to experience true happiness in a romantic relationship. With this limiting belief, despite a person striving to have positive and happy relationships in their life, they're unable to do so. This limiting belief may have taken root because of things like a first-hand experience or observation of other relationships around them.

> *"Life has no limitations, except the ones you make."*
> *—Les Brown*[8]

Another common limiting belief regarding romantic relationships is that the person themselves is not good enough to have success in relationships. This can lead to the person self-sabotaging relationships through actions like unnecessarily starting arguments, even if a positive and happy romantic relationship is what they truly want. Just as with money, these types of limiting beliefs can be working in exact contradiction to what it is that we really want in life.

Limiting beliefs will find a person making decisions and taking actions that go against what they want to achieve or attain. Consider this: Have you ever made a big decision that you later regretted? It could be anything—a break up, starting an argument with a spouse, ending a friendship, making a poor financial decision. Maybe, it was almost as if you knew it was wrong when you made the decision, but something deep in your mind was pushing you to do it anyway? That may have been a limiting belief speaking.

If you're still wondering whether you have a limiting belief—that's OK. Like we said, not all limiting beliefs are consciously apparent. Let's dig in a little here. In simplest terms, everything we think about can be categorized as either positive or negative. How you *feel* about the thought you're having will let you know whether it's a positive or a negative. Positive thoughts and feelings bring us closer to the things we want in life. Negative thoughts and feelings bring us further from the things we want in life. Positive thoughts and feelings bring about happiness. Negative thoughts and feelings bring about unhappiness.

Knowing that, try this: Think about money for a few minutes. Really think long and hard about the topic. Do you naturally *feel* positive or negative about it? Now, think about those you know who have a lot of money. Picture them on vacation. Picture them in their mansion. Picture them throwing elaborate parties and wearing expensive clothes. Does that make you *feel* positive or negative? If you're feeling positive about money all around, that's a good sign. What many may find is that they think their thoughts on money are positive, but the second they consider someone who has more money than them, the feeling of jealousy pops up. If *any* of the above makes you feel negative in any way—including any feelings of jealously—there is likely a limiting belief that exists.

If you feel good about money, that's great. Keep those positive feelings going as they will serve you well in life. If you feel negative about money, it's time to make a change—especially if it's a goal of yours to live with an abundance of money.

Are any realizations popping into your mind right now? Any "ah hah!" moments? If you're slowly uncovering a limiting belief, now is the time to break the chains and start living your happiest and most successful life. The first step is realizing what your limiting belief (or beliefs) is. The next step is committing to replace your current belief with a new, positive one.

> *"If we can see past preconceived limitations, then the possibilities are endless."*
> —*Amy Purdy*[8]

Here is a tried and true technique for those who are currently needing to alter a limiting belief. Take out a piece of paper and start to write down the things you are currently grateful for in your life. Keep writing until you reach at least five items on your list (hopefully, you'll be writing down a lot more than five!). Once you're done, look at each item on the list and think of each one closely. Think of how each of them makes you feel. You feel good, right?

Now, write about the topic on which you've uncovered a limiting belief. The point here is to begin changing the negative thoughts about the topic to positive thoughts about the topic. If our earlier money example rang true for you, try writing down a list of things you want financially as if you already have them. Examples may include, "I am grateful that I have all the money that I need," "I am grateful that I have financial security and independence," and "I am grateful that money is available to me anytime I need it." Write these items about money as if you are already in possession of them. Try to write down at least five of these items. You can have *all* these things in your lifetime—and more! (In an upcoming chapter, we're going to focus on goal setting, but for now it's a good idea to focus one-at-a-time on those items you've just written down. As you begin to achieve one, you'll find yourself moving on to achieve the next and adding to the list.)

Writing those items down in the present tense mixed in with the things you are currently grateful for blends new, positive thoughts on money with the good things that already exist in your life. Right there you have the beginnings of a new, positive belief about money. Trust us—with practice, it works!

Just by going through that simple exercise you will undoubtedly feel better about the topic. Now, we just need to give your mind time to believe it. The new belief will become stronger and stronger every time you do this exercise. This powerful exercise can start to send you in a different direction and start to form a new belief for you that can pay off handsomely over the course of your life.

Again, that exercise can be used on *any* topic. It works for changing all types of limiting beliefs to new, positive ones—if you mentally allow it.

Be patient with yourself. As we mentioned, some beliefs can be deep-rooted, and these may take a while to fully change. It's just like building a muscle. With consistent exercise, you can change your limiting beliefs and will, in turn, discover that your new beliefs will help lead you down a road to success.

> *"When you see your dream car, a happy couple, the perfect body, children, great qualities in a person, or whatever it is you want, it means you are on the same frequency as those things! Be excited, because your excitement is choosing it."*
> —*Rhonda Byrne*[9]

Later in the book, we'll talk about keeping an ongoing gratitude journal, but for now, you should consider trying that exercise every day for the next 30 days. We promise you it will take less than 10 minutes per day and will be greatly beneficial for you. If you don't have any limiting beliefs you feel need to be replaced, in the second section you can just simply write down things you want to achieve or attain as if they are already in your possession (again, focus on achieving one at a time). Watch closely as the direction of your life begins (or continues to) point in a positive direction just by doing this.

Once you've begun to change any limiting belief for the better, you may quickly find that things that in the past had felt unattainable to you are beginning to find themselves within reach.

> *"Don't limit yourself. Many people limit themselves to what they think they can do. You can go as far as your mind lets you. What you believe, remember, you can achieve."*
> —*Mary Kay Ash*[8]

Be aware that positive beliefs and positive thoughts alone will not always lead to success. A key component to that equation is *action*. We need to not only believe something is possible and think positively about it, we need to also put in the appropriate action in order to achieve success—it's vital. (For example, if you're single and have a goal of getting married and starting a family, you wouldn't sit home simply wishing for it to happen, right? You'd first want to make sure you're mentally thinking positively about the topic of relationships, and then you'd want to start taking an action of some sort to meet a romantic partner.)

We'll get into the action component in detail throughout the book. For now, just know that *the combination of believing strongly in something and taking action to achieve it is one that cannot be beat!*

CHAPTER 3

Creating a Positive Mindset

T he mind is a very powerful tool. Yet, most people do not know just how powerful it is, nor do they understand how to use the mind to get anything they want in life. And we mean *anything*.

Below is the best way we have heard of the power of the mind explained. It comes from Dr. Napoleon Hill, as it was told to him by Andrew Carnegie. Here is the essence of how he described the power of the mind in *The Master Key to Success:*[10]

You come into this world with the equivalent of two sealed envelopes.

The first envelope is marked 'Riches & Happiness.' This envelope contains all the riches & happiness that you may enjoy if you take possession of your own mind and direct it to ends of your own choice.

Taking possession of your own thoughts is the only thing that separates us from all other living species and also the only thing that we have complete & unchallengeable control over. The benefits that you will enjoy by taking possession of your own mind are:

1. Sound Health

2. *Peace of Mind*
3. *A Labor of Love of your own choice*
4. *Freedom from Fear & Worry*
5. *A Positive Mental Attitude*
6. *Material Riches of your own choice & quantity*

The second envelope is marked 'Penalties.' In this envelope lies the penalties if you neglect to take possession of your own mind and direct it toward what you want and away from what you don't want.

1. *Ill Health*
2. *Fear & Worry*
3. *Indecision & Doubt*
4. *Frustration & Discouragement throughout life*
5. *Poverty & Want*
6. *A flock of Evils: Envy, Greed, Jealousy, Anger, Hatred & Superstitions*

Naturally, you would want to choose envelope #1, right? That's just what you should do. Then, you can start to take possession of your own mind and receive the benefits you are entitled to.

Before you can begin any journey to success—whether it's personal, professional or academic—you must first understand the important role your own thoughts play in the process.

It's been said that people generally only use 10 percent of their minds, and that's probably true. This is because most people have never taken advantage of the power of Forces of Nature and the wonders they can do for our minds. These forces never vary and never deviate.

Forces of Nature keep the planets and stars aligned and make sure that night follows day, summer follows spring and that an oak tree grows from an acorn, for instance. These Forces of Nature exist within every atom of matter, including the human mind. Knowing and understanding the role they play when it comes to the mind is critical. Forces of Nature allow our minds to attract what we're thinking of. You've likely heard the phrase "like attracts like." When it comes to our thoughts, this is commonly known as the Law of Attraction. That's just what our minds are capable of, but often times people aren't taking full advantage of this tactic. If you realize the power your mind holds, you can use your thoughts to help you attract anything you want.

Have you noticed that there are some people you know in life who it seems everything always goes their way? On the other hand, have you noticed some people have nothing but negative things happen in their life, one thing after another?

The difference is in their thoughts. If their mind is telling them to expect good things to happen, good things will follow. If their mind is telling them to expect bad things to happen, bad things will follow.

Let's look at it this way:

If a farmer plants wheat in a field, what is going to grow? If he plants corn in a field, what will grow? If you plant an acorn, what will grow? Nature never deviates, right? It always produces what is sown.

When you plant thoughts in your mind, just like the farmer planting the seeds, those thoughts draw to you what it is that you've planted, whether it's good or bad. Every person on this planet is exactly where they are because of the sum of their thoughts to date. There are no exceptions. It's the Law of Attraction at work. It is just as strong as the law of gravity.

"Suppose a farmer has some land—and it's good, fertile land. The land gives the farmer a choice. He may plant in that land whatever he chooses. The land doesn't care what is planted. It's up to the farmer to make the decision. Remember, we are

comparing the human mind to the land, because the mind,
like the land, doesn't care what you plant. It will return what
you plant, but it doesn't care what you plant."
    —Earl Nightingale[11]

What you produce in your life is solely dependent on what thoughts you deliberately plant into your mind. We are going to teach you how to plant the right thoughts in your mind, how to cultivate the soil, and how to water it so you can later reap the harvest. Like the farmer, the results of the seeds planted are not immediate. We will teach you how to mix those thoughts with emotion to help bring you the results you desire as quickly as possible.

Each of us has been given complete control over one thing in our lives... our thoughts. You are now going to utilize this power to create what you want in your life, provided you learn how to guide those thoughts toward definite ends.

No person has ever achieved great success with a negative state of mind. Those who succeed in life are those who can see the benefit in everything that happens to them, no matter what. This is because they have trained their brains to do so. They have a positive mindset, always. They have learned, practiced and fully utilized the Law of Attraction to get what they desire. They know that positive thoughts and speech will attract positive circumstances and that negative thoughts and speech will attract negative circumstances. If they think and speak in a positive manner, they will get positive results every time.

As we recently mentioned, while so many things are beyond our own control in life, what we think and how we think about it is completely controlled by ourselves. Allowing yourself to come to that realization and then beginning to take control over your thoughts will be critical in achieving success now and throughout your entire life.

"If you think in negative terms, you will get negative results. If you think in positive terms, you will achieve positive results. That is the simple fact which is the basis of an astonishing law of prosperity and success. In three words: Believe and succeed."

　　—*Dr. Norman Vincent Peale*[12]

Maybe you already function in your daily life using a positive mindset and aren't even aware you're doing so. Some people seem to be born hard-wired to think of the positive in things versus the negative. Others, however, function quite the opposite. No matter where you stand today, a positive mindset is something you can attain simply by changing your thoughts and what you focus on. And, it will result in great success for you.

Let's think again about those people you know who always seem to get what they want and seldom seem to be faced with problems or difficulties. Now again think of those people you know who are faced with nothing but problem after problem. Consider the conversations you have had with each of these individuals. Do the conversations with the first person seem to be a lot more positive than the conversations you have with the second? It's very likely that is the case.

Consider your brain as a magnetic force. It attracts to you what you think and what you speak. If you're focused on the positive, positive things will be drawn to you. If you're focused on the negative, negative things will be drawn to you. It's really that simple. Many books have been written on the topic of the Law of Attraction, some based on countless years of research on the world's most successful people. The Law of Attraction is practiced by millions of successful people every day to get what it is they most desire in life.

A positive mindset enhances a person's confidence in their ability to succeed. It makes it so that the brain is so sure it will receive what it wants that it simply knows no other way.

For many people, there is an inherit force acting inside their mind that is working to only see the negative in situations and to fear and expect negative outcomes. The trick is to fight against this urge by continuously changing the negative thoughts to positive ones until that negativity no longer exists.

Let's consider the example of Curtis Jackson, more commonly known as "50 Cent"—a rapper, actor and entrepreneur. The practice of substituting negative thoughts for positive ones made an incredible difference for him.

50 Cent was born into poverty and raised by a single mother in a rough New York City neighborhood. His mom worked as a drug dealer and died in a fire when he was only eight years old. After her death, he was raised by his grandmother. He began selling drugs when he was just 12 years old, subsequently dropped out of school and was constantly in trouble with the law. At age 19, he was arrested for a serious drug dealing offense and landed himself in boot camp.

During his time there, he began to slowly get into the right mindset and studied to obtain his GED (General Educational Development certification – commonly known as the equivalent of a high school diploma). Following bootcamp and upon his return to New York City, he was shot multiple times and left for dead on the street. As he was in bed recovering from the gunshot wounds, he decided to permanently change his mindset from a negative one to a positive one, get away from his past life and pursue his dream of entering the entertainment business.

With that change of mindset, 50 Cent went from a life of poverty and trouble with the law to one of fame, success, and fortune. It all started with his enhanced way of thinking.[13]

Picture your mind like a river, with thoughts flowing downstream to a fork in that river. On one side flows the positive thoughts; the other, your negative thoughts. You can easily redirect the flow by building a mental dam on the negative side and allowing the thoughts to only flow into the positive side. It doesn't have to happen overnight. One small branch at a time to create that dam will slowly begin the process of redirecting negative thoughts to the positive side. As more branches and leaves start to accumulate on the negative side, all of a sudden *everything* begins to flow positive. All you have to do is start one by one, like the branches creating the dam, to replace a negative thought with a positive one. Little by little, day by day, you—like the positive side—will begin to flourish, while the negative side dries up.

"A positive attitude is a choice, like walking to the other side of a street to avoid trouble or making a 180-degree turn when you feel you're heading in the wrong direction."
—Richard M. DeVos[14]

Whether your mindset is currently positive or negative, all of us can benefit from following some of the below guidelines as a means of helping to create the most positive mindset possible for ourselves. Again, a positive mindset will result in success at every turn, because failure will not be an option. You will start to see things differently and will experience better relationships, better opportunities, more money and anything else you desire.

Leave Your Failures in the Past

To get started, consider any of your past failures you are mentally holding on to. Think long and hard to uncover them. Whether you think about these failures regularly or not, to some degree they are creating negative space in your brain. It is time to let them go and free up that space for positive thoughts and visualizations of the good things you want.

All of us have experienced failures in the past. Let's vow to leave them there... in the past. According to the Law of Attraction, focusing on past failures will only bring about more failures. We attract what it is we think about.

We simply don't have time for failure when we're ramping up to succeed. Come to terms with these failures, learn from them, then dismiss them from your mind and refocus to the present, with a positive eye on the future.

We know someone who, when being introduced to this concept, took the time to write down all of their past failures and regrets on a piece of paper, then took that paper, ripped it into tiny pieces, went into their yard and buried that ripped up paper. Her words when she returned from the yard were, "They are now buried for good, never to bother me again." This is a great way to literally bury your past failures, learn the lessons you need to from them and move on. You don't want to waste any moments of this precious life dwelling on the past.

Start Every Day on a Positive Note

Those who have a positive mindset start each and every day on a positive foot. Waking up on the wrong side of the bed is just a myth to them. They have trained their brain to wake up and immediately think positive thoughts, despite what may be happening in their life.

Gratitude has proven to be a great example of a positive way to begin your day and to set your mind on a positive path for the rest of the day. In the last chapter, we encouraged you to try the gratitude exercise every day for

30 days. Beyond that, you may want to consider keeping a gratitude journal, and writing in it every morning. Similar to our earlier exercise, write down five things you are grateful for every day. It will help to remind you of the blessings you have in your life and stop your mind from focusing on any issues or hurdles you imagine you may be faced with that day. Additionally, having all that you are grateful for written down will allow you to go back and reference the points over and over whenever you are feeling down or when you're facing a hurdle of any kind. It will also set your mind in the right direction to attract more things that you are grateful for.

As discussed in the previous chapter, a very effective add-on to this practice is to also write down the things you *will* be grateful for in the future, as if you already have them. If your goal is to become President at your company, for example, you might write down, "I am grateful that I am President of my company." It's essentially a manifestation exercise. As we've mentioned, when writing down the things you plan to be grateful for in the future, try focusing in on one at a time when working toward them. This will allow you the opportunity for enhanced focus.

Another example of how to start your day on a positive note is by beginning it with a good, hearty laugh. Listen to a funny podcast on your way to work or watch a funny YouTube video before you even get out of bed in the morning. This will help set a positive tone for the day.

Morning affirmations can also help. This exercise can help remind you that you can have whatever it is you want in life. You can also try saying aloud the things you want to achieve to verbally cement them. One example might be, "I am going to become President of my company! I am intelligent and capable."

Pay Attention to How You're Feeling About a Thought

Feelings can oftentimes overwhelm us in a negative way, but they do not have to if we're in control of our own mind. The trick here is to pay attention to what you are feeling. If a thought comes up and it makes you feel good, hold onto it. Think about it again, and again, and again. It means you're aligning yourself to something positive. Good results will follow.

Oppositely, if a thought you're having makes you feel negative, dismiss it. Get rid of it completely. It will only create that dreaded negative space in your brain and will serve you poorly. Simply substitute that negative thought with a positive one that makes you feel good and things will begin to change that instant.

You'll recall that how you feel about the thought you're having always tells you if you are heading in the right direction or not.

Every thought that comes into your mind regarding what you want out of life will either invoke a positive feeling or a negative feeling. This is because when your mind is thinking about something that will make you happy, you feel positive. Oppositely, when your mind is thinking about something that will make you unhappy, you feel negative. Therefore, thoughts such as "I cannot wait until I have a million dollars" will result in positive feelings and attract positive outcomes, and thoughts such as "I can't believe I still do not have a million dollars" will result in negative feelings and attract negative outcomes.

It's also very important to note that a positive and negative thought cannot occupy the mind simultaneously, so if a thought is negative, dismiss it and replace it with a positive thought. For instance, think of how happy you'll be when you achieve what it is that you want—and then keep focused there and move forward. It has been shown that thoughts that are emotionally-charged carry even greater power. So, carefully choose your thoughts and continuously monitor them by how you feel about that thought.

Look for the Silver Lining in All Negative Circumstances

"It's not the situation, but whether we react negative or respond positive to the situation that is important."
—*Zig Ziglar*[15]

You've likely heard the saying, "Everything happens for a reason," many times. For a lot of people, this is very hard to believe or wrap their head around. They'll deny that anything negative in their life—whether it's a big circumstance or a small one—has happened for any good purpose whatsoever. They can only see the good when positive things happen.

Everything *does* happen for a reason in the minds of those who have a positive mindset. This is because those with a positive mindset can see the positive in every situation that comes their way. They realize that, no matter what, if they look closely enough, they can find a benefit in every circumstance.

If you're like most people, your first reaction when something goes wrong is to get upset and/or frustrated. That is OK. That tends to be human nature. While you can't always avoid negative circumstances, you can, however, change the way you think about negative circumstances. This will help to better your mindset and set yourself up for future success. It takes practice, but it can be done.

In every negative circumstance, it is possible to find a benefit. Sometimes it may take some time to see it, but it is there. You can start practicing right now by thinking of a negative situation you're currently faced with and digging down deep to understand how this situation can be beneficial to you. Keep asking the question, "Where is the benefit in this?" Sooner or later, it will show up provided you keep asking the question and expecting the answer.

Then, from here on out, when a negative situation arises, stop in your tracks and think of the benefits that may be there. If you can't see it immediately, keep asking. Do this consistently and before you know it, your brain will automatically think of the benefits when faced with adversity without you even having to try. What you're doing through this exercise is conditioning your mind to attract and recognize beneficial results.

Granted, there will be times when benefits are extremely hard to come by in a situation. A good example of that is the death of a loved one. More often than not, when someone close to us passes away we cannot seem to wrap our heads around the rationale for it, let alone what a benefit could be. Certainly, there seems to be no immediate benefit, except in instances where the deceased is now out of pain. However, sometimes, even within very short time periods, the sorrow felt through this event can be converted into a benefit through a revived or new purpose.

The reflection time spent contemplating the life of the deceased or our own mortality, for instance, can bring inspiration to an individual beyond what had previously been there. Results can mean a new and improved attitude toward living every day to the best of their ability and enjoying it, newfound energy to make the deceased proud and/or dedicating good deeds to the deceased. Everyone has their own way of handling this situation; however, moving on with life, remembering the person in a positive light, and realizing our own mortality and the importance of making the most of time here on earth can set positive things in motion that will be of benefit to us.

Often when people are facing negative circumstances, they will simultaneously fear additional negative circumstances are likely to come their way soon. If you recognize this happening in your mind, stop the thought in its tracks and replace those thoughts with positive ones that make you feel good. Go back and grab a thought off the list of things you are grateful for and this will immediately start to change your mind from negative to positive. The fear of new negative circumstances will attract to you additional negative circumstances, as we know through the Law of Attraction.

You should expect positive things to happen in your life. This will, in turn, attract positive situations and outcomes.

It is a process to train your brain to think this way, so do not get discouraged if it takes you a while to get the hang of it. You will get there and it will change how you experience everything in your life.

Move on from Circumstances You Cannot Do Anything About

As discussed earlier, our thoughts are the only thing we can control. Throughout your life, there will be plenty of circumstances that will be out of your control, but how you think about them will dictate how they affect you. Let's say you're currently faced with a problem you cannot do anything about. Try this: Let it go. Move on. All that matters is that you do not let it negatively affect your mindset. Holding onto the problem and trying to resolve it when it cannot be resolved will prove to be a waste of time and a negative experience for you. Focus on the things you *can* do something about, and you will find that the things you cannot do something about will become unimportant– or will more easily resolve themselves—later on.

It's been said that when Henry Ford had a problem he could do nothing about, he would simply focus on the aspects of the problem that he could do something about, even if they were minor. By the time he revisited the bigger problem at hand, it was no longer even a problem at all.

> *"If you have a positive attitude and constantly strive to give your best effort, eventually you will overcome your immediate problems and find you are ready for greater challenges."*
> —*Pat Riley*[16]

Do Good by Others

Giving back to others is vital to achieving success. Doing good by others will set your mind in a positive state. Ask yourself, "Who can I help today?"

Even the smallest acts of kindness will make you feel good and more positive. Get started now by making a pact with yourself to do something nice for someone every day for a week. Again, it can be small (or large, if you have the capacity). Maybe today it's picking up an extra coffee on your way into work or school for someone else. Maybe tomorrow it's holding the door for someone. Maybe the next day it's helping a neighbor carry their groceries into their home.

Likewise, doing good for someone else might mean helping them to look for solutions to a problem they're having. Helping someone else solve their problem might open a new way of thinking for you to solve a problem you're facing as well. Look for opportunities to be helpful or do a nice deed and, we promise you, something positive will come out of it every time.

Make Peace with Those Who've Harmed You

Similar to how our past failures may be causing stagnant, negative space in our brains, without even realizing it, holding onto grudges or hard feelings against others can be doing the very same thing. This is because, whether these thoughts of frustration regarding another person are recent or front of mind for us or not, they are in fact there in our head taking up precious space. It's time to let them go.

To accomplish this, you may consider having a one-on-one conversation with whomever it is. This is not practical in all situations, however, so it is similarly OK to make peace within your own mind with the person and let it go, just as we did with our past failures. Make peace with it, wish them well and then block it out of your mind.

Surround Yourself with Like-Minded People

With a positive mindset, you'll want to surround yourself with others who also have a positive mindset. This will help to keep you on track. Because of the Law of Attraction, being positive will naturally attract to you others of a similar mindset. However, this doesn't always mean the negative people in our lives won't be there still. We just have to be aware of how to properly manage our interactions with these individuals.

As with other guidelines we've discussed, this can be easier said than done. Many of us might find that people we live with, people we work with, people we're friends with, and so on, are negative. What should we do? Try this: For every negative thing they have to say, counter it with something positive, or simply ignore it. They can talk endlessly about a negative topic, but don't let it affect you. Don't let it into your mind.

A great technique for listening to people who are negative if you absolutely have to is to build an imaginary wall in your mind. While they continue to talk about negative topics and circumstances, simply envision a wall that is built in your mind that does not allow what they are saying to enter or have any effect on you. Your mind is your greatest and most precious asset, so do not allow others who are not in harmony with you to enter. Protect it at all costs.

Keep Your Mind Busy

An idle mind can quickly become a negative mind. Why is this? Because lack of stimulating mental activity can cause you to overthink and overanalyze situations that may have otherwise gone unnoticed by your brain—and many times that overthinking results in you finding the negative in situations.

The busier your mind is, the more positive it will be. Staying mentally busy could include continuing to practice the guidelines we've previously mentioned, participating in a hobby you enjoy, furthering your education in some way, and more. As it's been said, "An idle mind is the devil's workshop."

Consider the farmer example again. A farmer who plants his crop and then takes proper care of the soil and its surrounding conditions will yield the best harvest. Oppositely, if he plants his crop and neglects to do anything else to it, it will yield a poor harvest. When it comes to your mind, tend to it properly by taking action to keep it positive and you will reap the harvest. Otherwise, by neglecting it, the weeds of negativity will take over.

Pay attention and you'll quickly notice that the less idle your brain is, the more positive your outlook on life will be.

Visualize Where You Want to Be... and Get There!

Anything you can conceive in your mind is possible to achieve. It begins within your own thoughts. You must be able to mentally visualize getting where you want to go and how you'll get there. At all times, you should have your mind preoccupied with what you want. It should drive everything you do, even the smallest of tasks throughout a day. See yourself living the life you want and you will have it.

The problem most people face is that they continually are visualizing the things they do not want instead of visualizing the things they do want. Use the power of your mind to do just the opposite.

> *"The greatest discovery of my generation is that human beings can alter their lives by altering their attitudes of mind."*
> *—William James*[17]

Remind Yourself Repeatedly That Success is the Only Option

You will be successful in any venture personally, professionally or academically if your mind knows success is the only option. How will it know this to be true? You have to tell it so. And, you have to do so repeatedly. In the next chapter we talk about the importance of repeating your goal and your plan to achieve it and keeping it front of mind. You should tell yourself regularly that you will succeed in achieving this goal. Say it again. And again. And again. Say it with feeling. Believe you will achieve what you want and stay focused—it's an irresistible power.

Without a positive mindset, it will be very difficult to achieve success in any area of your life. Now that we fully understand how a positive mindset correlates to success, let's figure out what exactly it is that you want out of life, and let's help you get it.

CHAPTER 4

Taking Action Through Goal Setting and Planning

Now that you have a clear understanding of the vital role your mind plays in achieving success, it's time to talk about the other key component to achieving success: Taking action. We briefly mentioned earlier how having the right beliefs and a positive mindset—when coupled with action—is a combination that cannot be beat. Well, it's true! Both your mindset and the actions you're willing to take to get want you want play equally important roles.

Let's go back for a second to an example we used at the end of Chapter 2 on limiting beliefs. Let's say you are single and your goal is to get married and start a family. To you, that will equate to living a happy and successful life. So, you uncovered a limiting belief about relationships, replaced it with a new, positive belief through our gratitude exercise, but now what? Do you sit back without taking action and just wish that you will meet a romantic partner? No way. You need to also *do* something about it. You'll need to take some action—whether that means joining an online dating site, asking a friend to set you up on a date with someone they know, going to a speed dating event, speaking to more people when you're out in public—whatever action feels right and comfortable to you. By adding in that action element, you will begin to quickly see how things progress for you.

Now, let's really delve into this action piece some more. It all begins with setting a goal for yourself—and is followed up with developing a plan of action to achieve it. Remember, anything is possible with the right mindset.

"Whatever the mind can conceive and believe it can achieve."
—Dr. Napoleon Hill[18]

First, let's note here that to find success at anything in life you must determine exactly what it is you want to achieve. You *must* have a goal outlined. A goal allows you to set a clear intention and establish a purpose.

You and only you have the power to deliberately create the life that you want—but to do so, you must be deliberate about it!

Consider your goal as something you can get really excited about. Your goal can be personal, professional, something relevant to your education, or a combination of all of them—really it is whatever you want it to be. If you're initially drawing a blank, refer back to the lists you were making through your gratitude exercise from earlier chapters. What was the main item you wanted to focus in on to achieve? That may very well be your goal.

To live *your* most successful life, your goal should be something *you* want to achieve, not something someone else is encouraging you to achieve. Remember, just as only you can define what happiness means to you, only you can define what success means to you as well.

Once you've decided on what your goal will be, start to imagine yourself already having achieved it. Imagine the happiness you'll feel along the journey to achieving it, too.

Remember again that achieving what one wants out of life involves not only having the right beliefs and a positive mindset, but—quite importantly—also a person's ability to define and take action to achieve one's goal.

You have heard plenty of success stories in your lifetime. Think closely of some of them for a moment. Steve Jobs. Thomas Edison. Mark Zuckerberg. Bill Gates. Did the success of any of these figures fall in their laps? The answer to that is simple: No. Each of these individuals, and anyone else who has achieved their own success, did so by first determining what they wanted to achieve and then taking action to achieve it.

"All our dreams can come true if we have the courage to pursue them."
—Walt Disney[19]

It may take time to define exactly what you want, but once you do, achieving it is controlled by the power of your own mind. And, it is followed by the appropriate actions set in motion to achieve it. Anything can be achieved when focused on properly.

Many people simply think of the things they want out of life and sit by idly wishing they will happen. Wishes don't result in the achievement of meaningful success.

Everyone wishes for things. We wish for more money, better relationships, better grades in school, and the like. When we wish for them, we don't define specifics around the wish, nor do we consider the action plan that will be needed in order to have the wish fulfilled. Instead, we passively sit back and wait for it to come to us without planning or effort. A wish is something a genie would grant—the likelihood of getting it is almost fairy tale-like. If, per chance, a wish is granted on a whim, it will not be as meaningful to us as if we'd earned it ourselves.

Success as we're talking about it in this book is something you're going to earn. You're going to need to work hard for it, but we assure you, the results are going to be well worth it. Nothing is going to stand in your way of achieving success. Absolutely nothing.

It's important for you to translate what may have otherwise been a wish into a clearly-defined goal. It should be as detailed as possible and should be something you're *obsessed* with wanting to achieve. The more obsessed you are with achieving the goal, the more of your mental space it will take up. You'll want to achieve it so badly that you seemingly won't be able to stop thinking about it. You'll find yourself repeating it over and over in your head throughout the day.

Working toward achieving that goal will not be a passive thing. It will be very active and will require—and should receive—a lot of attention.

> *"A man is what he thinks about all day long."*
> *—Ralph Waldo Emerson*[20]

As we've mentioned, your goal should be a goal for yourself—not something that someone else wants for you. Your goal should be something that will make you happy. When it's your goal and you feel good about it, it won't seem like work as you move toward its attainment, but rather it will become a labor of love for you, and you will want to spend your time moving toward reaching it.

When defining a goal, specifics should include things like quantity and a timeframe for when you would like to achieve it by. Your goal should be written down and repeated over and over until it's the primary, driving force for why you do nearly everything you do in life.

Take some time to think right now of what your goal will be. Again, define specifics. For example, "I will earn $2 million within the next 10 years" or "I will have a mansion on the beach by age 30," or "I will get accepted to the University of Pennsylvania."

What do you want? What will bring you joy (not only once it's achieved, but also on the path to achieving it)? What do you desire your life to be like? Anything is possible.

Are you a tech person hoping to launch a start up? Are you looking to make it in the acting world? Trying to lose a certain amount of weight in a certain timeframe? As you're thinking through this, remember the importance of being as specific as possible with what you want and when you want to achieve it.

Then, stop for a minute here once the goal is defined and visualize yourself having already achieved the goal. Keep that visualization in your mind. Do not waver. The feeling you're having is good, right? If not, take that as a hint that that goal is not for you.

> *"Take responsibility of your own happiness. Never put it in other people's hands."*
> *—Roy T. Bennett*[21]

While much of this book is focused on achieving a larger, more significant goal for yourself—something big that you want to achieve in your lifetime—you can always use this blueprint for success to achieve smaller, short-term goals as well. It is all up to you to determine what it is you want to achieve. Next, it's planning time.

Just as important as setting the goal for yourself is creating a plan to get you there. The plan should also be specific and written down. It should include necessary steps you will need to take and appropriate deadlines, as well as specifics on any areas that may require help from others. Keep in mind that not all goals can be achieved by a person alone. In fact, more times than not, achievement of our goals requires assistance from other people. Do not be afraid to ask people for help. Importantly, make sure they are an expert in the area you're asking them for help in so you can be assured they're heading you in the right direction.

Just how you'll remind yourself daily of your goal, you should remind yourself regularly of the steps needed to get there. Think of your plan as a GPS guiding you to your destination.

Consider this way of looking at it. You're visiting New York City for the first time. You decide you're going to walk from your current location to a destination across town. Considering you have never been there and are unfamiliar with the city, would you walk without first looking up directions or using your phone's GPS to help guide you? To get to your destination most seamlessly, you would need to have it mapped out. This is how you should think about your plan for achieving your goal—like a GPS to guide you. Success will be nearly impossible without it. And it will be far easier to navigate roadblocks and obstacles with your GPS in hand.

Your plan can and should be flexible enough to change along the way. As you're moving through the steps, if a hurdle comes up, simply redirect as your GPS would do. All you need to do is ensure that—while your plan of achieving your goal may change—your goal itself, just like your destination with the GPS, should remain the same.

What if your plan doesn't work? What if you've come up with what you believe to be a reasonable plan, you've executed it and made changes along the way, and after much time you're still not making progress toward achieving your goal. Now what? This may simply mean there is a better plan for you. It is OK to revise your plan as needed. But stay with the goal and have faith in yourself that you will accomplish it.

Realizing those reading this book will have goals that vary greatly, we will not get into more detail about the specifics of developing a plan since, in turn, plans will vary greatly as well. That said, there are many books out there that can help guide you through planning for your specific goal. Likewise, it may be in your best interest to tap someone you know who has expert knowledge relevant to your goal to seek their advice on planning.

There is no goal that you are able to conceive for yourself that you are not able to achieve. The preceding sentence is worth reading again and taking a moment to think about.

Let's look at Thomas Edison as an example. Throughout his lifetime, he had more than 1,000 inventions, many of which he failed at countless times (his plan didn't work) before finally accomplishing them. He was known for his persistent attitude about accomplishing a goal, even when that meant that his plan needed to change. In fact, he was so persistent, that when inventing the light bulb—one of his most valued inventions—he failed over 10,000 times.

Yes, it is true. Thomas Edison failed over 10,000 times before successfully creating the light bulb. Astounding, right?[22]

Could he have given up at any point along the road? Absolutely. However, he refused to do so because defeat was not an option. He had a goal, fixed it in his mind, and altered his plan as necessary to achieve it. He did not stop until he did so. And, imagine just how different our world would be today without his persistence to come up with such instrumental inventions—and without the persistence of others throughout history who used the same mentality to succeed no matter what.

Your mind should begin to think of your goal as absolutely achievable, no matter what comes in its way. This mindset will deflect naysayers from outside, as well as any negative thoughts from within your own mind.

It may seem too simple to be true, but be assured this has worked time, and time, and time, and time again for the world's most successful people in history. The power of the brain in reaching success is unmatched. The key is to visualize and be both deliberate and persistent about what you want and how you will achieve it—and then making it happen.

It is estimated that 98 percent of people have not clearly defined their goal. While this large majority of the population is perhaps setting and achieving smaller goals throughout life (perhaps ones they need to at a job they do not like, for example, or a goal that another person is pushing them to achieve) they have not achieved great success simply due to the lack of big-picturing thinking, personal goal-setting and planning, and the use of the power of a positive mindset. Many times, these individuals lack the necessary confidence in themselves and end up selling themselves short on their goals, assuming they need to accept whatever life hands to them. If you've been thinking that way, it's time to take back control!

This book is set out to teach you how to be one of the 2 percent who will find success and achieve all it is that you want in life.

Think it and you can achieve it. Envision yourself already having achieved it. What does that look like? Burn that image into your mind.

For one particular athlete, LeBron James, he literally wrote it on his skin. Early on when James was just a junior in high school, it had already become apparent that he was destined for success in the basketball world. Sports Illustrated wrote a cover story on him at the time and titled it, "The Chosen One." His mind was so fixed on his goal of becoming the best that he got a tattoo across his back saying "Chosen One" as a reminder of who he was and where he was going. Success was not guaranteed for him at that point, but mentally he knew no other option but to succeed from there. And, that he did. With a cannot fail attitude, he became one of the most celebrated basketball players of all time.[23]

Examples from years of success stories have always shown certain attributes to be true of successful people. As you're beginning your personal journey to success by goal setting and planning, keep these things in mind:

1. **Successful people don't view what they are doing as work.** Rather, they view their work as a labor of love. They pursue what it is that they are striving for with enthusiasm. They are happy where they are and eagerly anticipate the next step and the achievement of their goal(s).

2. **Successful people are able to quickly and effectively make decisions.** Because they are always focused on their goal, successful people know they need to react quickly to the decision-making process in order to keep things moving forward. With a goal firmly in their mind, it's easy for them to make decisions. They simply ask themselves, "Is this taking me toward my goal, or not?" The decision is made not only quickly, but they are also made firmly. Successful people do not go back and forth on a decision. Rather, they make a decision and stick to it.

3. **Successful people keep their eyes peeled for opportunity.** As they're following their plan to achieve their goal, successful people are always looking at and considering opportunities that can allow them to meet their goal quicker or in a larger capacity than originally imagined.

4. **Successful people live in a "can do" world, not a "can't do" world.** To those who are successful, the idea of something being impossible is, well… impossible. They believe anything the mind can imagine can be achieved. Negative thoughts do not enter their minds and if they do, they are quickly dismissed and replaced with a positive thought, because they understand that both a positive and negative thought cannot exist in the mind at the same time. Essentially, failure is not an option.

5. **Successful people remain focused on their goal.** Despite the fact that plans to achieve your goal may change along the way, successful people will not deviate from the goal they've

established. The more the mind has focused on that goal and set out ways to achieve it, the more likely they will be to achieve it. More often than not, when a successful person achieves their goal, they are then apt to set and achieve a new goal. It's an on-going process for them.

6. **Successful people do more than is expected of them in all situations.** Doing more than is expected is a shining attribute of successful people. They tend to extend help to those around them and consider things that are beyond what is beneficial for themselves. They also tend to put in extra effort when it comes to work as well, beyond what is required of them.

7. **Successful people put in continuous effort.** Just how defining a goal was not a passive exercise, working toward achieving the goal is not a passive exercise either. A successful person's goal and plan are part of their day, each and every day. Effort is put in at every possible moment in order to reach success.

If you're still having trouble coming up with exactly what it is you want to achieve in life, either long-term or short-term, consider this exercise: Spend some time and write out an autobiography of your life as if you're writing it at the end of your lifetime. Look back and reflect on the big accomplishments you hope to have had at that point and detail them thoroughly. It doesn't have to be an entire novel or take up too much of your time if you don't want it to. Even a short and simple version of this exercise can prove very helpful in pointing you toward what you want. From there, a plan to achieve it will begin to fall into place.

Once you have clearly defined your goal and have defined your plan to achieve it, you can also develop smaller purposes and goals, particularly those that lead you in the direction of your initial goal. As with your initial goal and plan, be sure to write down any supplementary goals. Repeat these over and over in your head as you've done with your initial goal until the brain knows nothing other than that it will achieve these things.

CHAPTER 5

Building Your Inner Faith

"Believe in yourself! Have faith in your abilities! Without a humble but reasonable confidence in your own powers you cannot be successful or happy."
—*Dr. Norman Vincent Peale*[24]

F aith. It's a word that translates to many different things for many different people. Upon hearing the word "faith," we often immediately think of religious beliefs specifically. Some people reading this book may follow a specific religion and others may not follow any religion at all—so when you see that this chapter is about faith, maybe you're hesitant to read and follow what it says.

Fear not, however. This chapter is *not* intended in the least to sway your current religious (or lack thereof) beliefs. Our discussion here on faith does not need to correlate to a religion at all, if that's not applicable to you. In fact, here we're going to delve into why *having faith in yourself* that you can achieve anything you want in life is going to significantly increase your ability to achieve it. It's been shown time and time again to work—so let's see how to monopolize on it.

As we've learned, in the very large majority of cases, things aren't just going to happen without putting in any work. Many people spend their life simply wishing for the things they want, and not putting any effort behind it. Our goals are only achieved through a positive mindset followed by action. It's not a passive process.

So far, we know that the work that needs to go into making anything achievable in life begins with eliminating any limiting beliefs and creating a positive mindset for ourselves. From there, we must determine what exactly is it that we want and a plan to achieve it. Inner faith now becomes an important ingredient to the mix. Faith gives life to your plans and desires. We're sure you would agree with us on this: If you do not believe you're able to achieve what it is that you want, you will never be able to actually achieve it. Faith must be demonstrated—and must be done so daily.

"Desire, backed by faith, knows no such word as impossible."
—Dr. Napoleon Hill[25]

Inner faith, in our terms, refers to belief in yourself. It is the belief that you can accomplish your desires. The application of inner faith in your thoughts, conversations and actions is crucial to achieving success of any kind.

Many people believe in the old statement, "I'll believe it when I see it." The way we should all really be thinking about it is, "I'll see it when I believe it."

Building inner faith in yourself is done primarily in a two-fold manner. The first is eliminating the fears that may be holding you back. Similar to how a positive thought and a negative thought cannot occupy your mind at the same time, faith and fear cannot occupy your mind at the same time either. This is why fear of not achieving a goal can lead to a person not achieving a goal—there is no room for faith where fear exists. You must work to identify what that fear may be and eliminate it immediately.

There are many topics that can cause fear in people and ultimately hold people back from living their most successful life. These fears can often present themselves in areas that have a direct connection to a person's happiness and/or goal(s). Money is a great example. For instance, a person may live in fear that they will not be able to pay their bills every month. Perhaps this person fears they'll never be able to have a job that pays them a surplus of cash—perhaps because they are not skilled enough or do not have the proper education. What is this fear and negative way of thinking going to do? It's going to reinforce these notions into a person's mind that they are incapable and prevent them from achieving a state of financial comfort. The fear itself directly counteracts what the person so desires—to be able to *afford* to pay bills. See how fears can work against you?

> *"Every day, in every way, I'm getting better and better."*
> —*Émile Coué*[26]

If you fear a lack of money, it will draw a lack of money to you... it's the Law of Attraction at work again. So, if you find yourself with fears relevant to money, all you need to begin doing is re-grounding by seeing yourself in possession of the material things you desire and standing tall in expectation that they will be yours. If thoughts related to this fear enter your mind, replace the "lack" thought with one of expectation to gain. As you practice this over and over, eventually the "lack of" thought will be permanently replaced by thoughts of faith that you will receive what you're asking for. Then you are sure to receive it.

Another common fear people have is related to a perceived lack of time. We often hear of this fear in those in the latter half of their life, but this fear could be applicable to anyone. Either way, it diminishes faith—so it needs to be eliminated if you're hoping to build your inner faith and achieve what you want. If you're someone who fears their goal will take too long to achieve and that's it's impossible to achieve in your lifetime, once again your negative thoughts on this will make it so. In a future chapter we'll cover in detail a range of time management practices, but for now it's important to realize that time should not be something you fear. In fact, it should be something that works for you. We guarantee you that with proper time management and the use of the other lessons we're covering throughout this book, you have plenty of time to achieve what you want out of life. You just need to put this fear aside and have faith.

> *"You can't help getting older, but you don't have to get old."*
> *—George Burns*[27]

On a more general note, some people tend to live their life with an underlying fear that things will not work out for them. Perhaps they've watched how others around them have failed in finding happiness and success, so they constantly live in fear that this will be their fate as well. If you're someone who has this general fear, it is likely you'll find yourself regularly saying things like, "I'm just waiting for the other shoe to drop." You live in fear that the worst will happen or that negative circumstances are around the corner, and just like that, you get just want you mentally envisioned. At the core, you're lacking any faith whatsoever.

For some people, that general fear feels oddly comforting. They feel as though by anticipating and expecting the worst results and living in fear of them, they're preparing themselves for potential let down. They won't feel blindsided at a negative circumstance because they've already mentally prepared themselves for it to happen. While we see how this could appear on the surface like a good tactic when viewed that way, what this is really doing is continuing to attract negative results rather than attracting positive results.

By eliminating this type of general fear and instead making a point to always expect good results, we'll find ourselves receiving good results. There is an old saying that tells us to expect the best and be prepared for the worst. Being prepared for the worst in this sense is not sitting idly in fear, though. It's keeping our eyes on the prize and being willing to adapt our plan to achieve our goal should a hurdle arise.

Now that we've discussed some fears that can hold you back from building inner faith, we can focus on the second component of building faith in yourself which is learning to put your faith into action and applying it to whatever you want in life.

Putting faith into action begins first with having a clear goal and plan in mind. As we've discussed, you will always find the most success if you're focused on exactly what it is you want and how you'll get there. When you're reminding yourself of your goal each day, for instance, and thinking positively about how to find success with it, you're building your inner faith that you're going to make it happen. Every time you tell yourself it will happen, your faith in yourself grows more and more.

Another important way you can put your faith into action is by remembering to regularly show gratitude each day. This is another place where your gratitude journal will continue to benefit you. If you haven't started your gratitude journal yet, now may be the time!

For those who follow a religion, here is your opportunity to connect your religious faith to your inner faith and your ability to achieve your goal. Often when people pray, it is because they are asking for something. If you're someone who prays, use that opportunity to show gratitude and thanks first and foremost. Build in a few extra minutes of your prayer time to give thanks for the blessings you already have in your life and then to reaffirm your faith in yourself that you will achieve your goal. You must *give* gratitude before you can expect to *receive* what you want.

If you're not religious, then simply practice this on your own. Prayer is not a required step here. All that matters is that you're remaining positive, focused and grateful for what you have already. With this in place, your inner faith will flourish.

We've also mentioned in previous chapters that surrounding yourself with like-minded people will benefit your ability to succeed. Building your faith is no different. If you're constantly surrounding yourself with naysayers who are crippling your faith in yourself and reminding you of those fears you're working hard to eliminate, this can have negative effects of many kinds. Where possible, avoid those with a negative mindset and who lack faith in themselves and diminish your inner faith. Instead, surround yourself with those who live their life with a positive mindset, with faith grounding them, and those who help you to build your faith in yourself.

Consider this example of Thomas Edison. According to Edison, when we was young he overheard a teacher saying that he was "addled" and that it would not be worth keeping him in school anymore.[28] *He went home crying and told his mother about it. She immediately came to her child's defense—marching down to the school and telling the teacher that he had no idea what he was talking about. Her child was brilliant! Edison said from that point he knew he needed to prove his mother right.*

And that he did. With his mother's reassurance and inner faith in himself, he discovered more of nature's secrets in his lifetime than had previously been discovered by anyone else since the beginning of the human race.[29]

This example shows us how important it is to instill faith, not only in yourself, but in others as well.

"Believe in yourself, and the rest will fall into place. Have faith in your own abilities, work hard, and there is nothing you cannot accomplish."

—Brad Henry[30]

Be patient with yourself as you work through this process of building your inner faith. Building faith in yourself can and will take time. The concept is quite similar to how creating a positive mindset will take time (you will quickly see how the two work hand-in-hand). Continue to practice the building of your inner faith on a daily basis. After a while, that faith will be engrained in you and nothing can stop you from fulfilling your goal.

CHAPTER 6

Doing More Than Is Expected

I f you are willing to give more than is expected of you in a given situation, you will benefit, every time. This concept is tried and true. Just as you've begun to engrain positive thoughts and actions into your daily life, and as you're starting to build your inner faith, you must also begin to engrain the habit of doing more than is expected of you. Collectively, this will all point you to success, without a doubt.

At this point in the book, you should thoroughly understand why establishing and maintaining a positive mindset is so crucial to achieving your goals. The things that we think and say are literally being put out into the universe, and the universe is going to respond accordingly. We're able to receive the things we want to receive in life depending on whether our thoughts and spoken words remain positive and whether or not we take corresponding action. That's a matter of fact and has been proven many times. We're certain of it.

Doing more than is expected of us in our personal and professional lives allows just the same type of reaction from the universe. These positive actions on our part can be considered to work the same way as our positive thoughts. Every time we give more than is expected in a situation of any kind, we can expect a positive return. It's a simple concept, however for many, it requires much patience and practice to conquer. Why? Well, for one, it's way easier to just do the minimum in situations, right?

For those who are willing to take the time to learn, practice and implement this habit, you will find sooner or later that doors are opening everywhere for you. Your path to success will come easier, no matter what your goals are.

We should mention here that doing more than is expected of you can translate to anything—maybe it's volunteering at a homeless shelter or taking on a new extra-curricular project at school. Maybe it's raising your hand to take on a new project at work that's outside of your job description. Maybe it's doing a favor for a friend.

> *"Do more than is required. What is the distance between someone who achieves their goals consistently and those who spend their lives and careers merely following? The extra mile."*
> *—Gary Ryan Blair*[31]

Doing more than is expected will result in returns that are far greater for you than you even imagined. Each and every time you do so, you are setting yourself up to receive more and more. Let's look at this closely from a work perspective for a moment.

Try to visual yourself in this situation: You've just started a new job and you have a goal for yourself to get a promotion, including a title and salary increase, within a year's time. How would you go about doing so? Would you do the bare minimum, or less than the minimum, in an effort to achieve this goal? The answer is no, right? Rather, you would do whatever you can to exceed the expectations of your employer to show him or her that the services you are providing are worthy of a higher title and pay grade. This might mean staying extra hours at the office and/or taking on additional projects and tasks that go above your job requirements. Point blank—if you have not been doing more than is expected of you, you will not have a leg to stand on when making the argument to get promoted.

Let's consider a friend of ours who experienced this firsthand. She worked in a mid-level position at a large health care organization making an average salary. For more than two years, she did more than was expected of her every day. She came in early, stayed late and handled responsibilities beyond her pay grade. She went above and beyond her call of duty and she desired to grow within the company.

One day she discovered a new position had become available that was not just a one-level advancement, but two levels higher than her current role and was accompanied by a very attractive salary. When she applied for the position, one of the organization's top executives immediately recognized her for the outstanding work and her ongoing willingness to do more than was expected of her. She was hired for the new position immediately. Going above and beyond, even when you don't think anyone is watching, always pays off.

If you give more, you are bound to receive more. For many people, it is the easier option to simply do what is required of them in situations, and nothing more. Instead of putting out the maximum effort, most will complain they've been passed over for a promotion or didn't receive a raise and will wonder why. This means that by understanding and applying this habit of doing more in situations, you will immediately stand out from the masses. You've become unique immediately.

"It's never crowded along the extra mile."
—Wayne Dyer[32]

Likewise, in the workplace, every time you are doing more than is expected of you, you are simultaneously making yourself indispensable.

"If you want to succeed at any job, make yourself invaluable. Go the extra mile; make them never be able to imagine what life without you there would be like."
– Ross Mathews[33]

Likely, there are many people who can provide the services you provide in the workplace. Doing more than is expected of you, while others in your field do the minimum, clearly and definitely helps you stand out among the crowd. People will remember your actions and gain further respect for you. They will know that—of all the people who have the skills to do your job—you will be the one to do it with the most effort. Instantly, you've become unique again.

Consider this example about the importance of becoming indispensable: Doug McMillon, current president and CEO of Walmart, began his time at the company when he was just a teenager. The hourly position had him loading trucks at a distribution center.

Over the years he consistently stayed with the company—moving from a role as an assistant store manager to a buyer trainee. He became truly indispensable to the company as he continued to climb the ladder and took on senior management roles in all of Walmart's business segments. By doing this, he was equipping himself with knowledge of the company across all of its areas, setting him apart from others who worked there who had only familiarized themselves with certain parts of the business. He took risks to set himself apart from others and it worked! His knowledge and experience became quickly invaluable from there, and it wasn't long before he landed the president and CEO position at the age of 47—the youngest CEO the company has had since its founder Sam Walton.[34]

If you're willing and able to do more than is expected of you—all while maintaining a positive mindset—it can easily lead to monetary or personal gain, can help you to be better liked by others, help further develop your sense of imagination, and much more.

Dr. Napoleon Hill taught two very important concepts relevant to this topic that are worth mentioning. First, he taught of what he called "The Law of Increasing Returns."[35] According to this law, every time you do more than is expected of you it will come back to you... without exception. Sometimes, the return will take some time to reveal itself—and sometimes it will come from an unexpected source—but it will *always* show up. A great thing about this law is that, according to Dr. Hill, not only can you expect returns every time, but they will often be even bigger than what you had done in the first place. As long as you're doing more than is expected of you without greed—and as long as you're continuing to maintain a positive mindset—you can expect the Law of Increasing Returns to work in your favor.

Secondly, Dr. Hill taught of "The Law of Compensation."[35] Essentially this law states that the more service you provide and the better you provide it, the higher you will be compensated (compensation here can be monetary but does not have to be). The idea here is that the harder you work to do more than is expected of you, the more you will receive in return. See how these two laws from Dr. Hill go hand-in-hand? See how they can benefit you?

Often people can become frustrated in their professional lives, specifically, when they believe they are going above and beyond and not being monetarily compensated fairly for it. Just as with the Law of Increasing Returns, patience is also required here. If after much time a person feels like they are still not receiving the compensation they deserve based on the work they're providing, it may simply be time to seek a different employer, and that's OK too. Remember that no matter what, if you're someone who is willing to go above and beyond with a positive mindset, returns will be coming to you!

By implementing this practice of doing more than is expected of you, you will unknowingly be building self-respect for yourself and your confidence will begin soaring. This is because you will know that, no matter the situation, you are also someone who goes beyond the call of duty and gives everything they have.

Now that we understand the reasons and benefits behind why we should always be aiming to do more than is expected, let's consider some ways you can begin implementing this practice in your life right now.

"If you want to lift yourself up, lift up someone else."
—Booker T. Washington[36]

Ask, "Who Can I Help Today?"

Is there someone in your life who you know is struggling in one way or another with a problem that is bigger than anything you're facing? Try carving out some time to help them in whatever means you can. This does not always need to translate to monetary assistance; it can be assistance of any kind, even emotional. By helping someone else overcome their problem, it will, without a doubt, come back to you with a positive return. For example, your help on someone else's problem may begin to open your mind on finding a solution to a problem you, yourself, are currently facing.

Remember, you should regularly be asking yourself, "Who can I help today?"

Perform Small Acts of Kindness for a Week

Another good way to begin implementing this habit is performing one small act of kindness every day for seven days in a row. These acts of kindness can be incredibly minor, such as holding the door open for someone or bringing a cup of coffee to a coworker in the morning. It can also include more professional acts of doing more than is expected, such as staying longer hours at work, tutoring someone at school, or volunteering for a new project, as mentioned in previous examples.

Improve on One of Your Own Skills

Another way to exercise this habit is to do so with an eye on self-improvement. Consider a task you do regularly and make it a point to do it better than you ever have done. Again, this can be either professional or personal. On this point, you can also consider things others are doing around you, let's say at work or school, and make it a point to try to do the task in a better way than others, further deeming yourself indispensable in the workplace or classroom.

Consider another example of the habit of doing more than is expected, as demonstrated by a man from Florida. At about the age of 30, Don was hired to run a self-storage facility. The job paid only about $25,000 per year and came with a small one-bedroom apartment over the storage facility's office. Don moved in with his wife, Tiffany, who was working part time and going to school. The business was floundering and had been purchased by a new owner when Don was hired. While the new owner knew much about real estate in general, he knew very little about the self-storage business. But, Don did.

The new owner's goal was to turn the facility around and produce a strong monthly cash flow, and accordingly, increase the value of the asset. During the first meeting with the new owner, the young man listened carefully to the owner's goal, expectations and plans. Without having to be asked to do so, immediately after the meeting Don began to draft his own plan to accomplish the owner's desires. The next week he presented the owner with a step-by-step, month-by-month plan that actually exceeded the owner's expectations. The plan was implemented and within a few months the facility began to show a profit. Within 18 months, it became so profitable that it was now worth $1,000,000 more than what the owner had paid (double the value).

Don was promoted and the owner went and acquired more self-storage facilities for him to operate. By this time, the owner realized the value of this young man and tied him into the profits of each new operation, and he was promoted again to Vice President. From there, they've partnered on many new facilities, where Don now owns a major stake.

Within six years, Don and Tiffany, now a CPA and Chief Financial Officer of the company, went from living in that small, one-bedroom apartment over the first storage facility to living in a 5,000 square foot mansion on several acres in a very upscale area. The couple are now millionaires. This is heavily due to the fact that they consistently did more than was expected of them. They planned and executed those plans to perfection, putting the company's best interests before their own. Now, they are rewarded many times over.

Remember, at the end of the day, the easiest path for a person to take is always going to be the one that requires the least amount of effort. That said, many people are simply not going to implement this habit of doing more than is expected because it's just too difficult—they want to make things easy on themselves. They'd prefer to do what is required of them, and nothing more.

Just by making it a point to implement this lesson into your life, you are guaranteed to stand out in the crowd and reap the rewards in every aspect of your life. With patience and a positive mindset, this will be beneficial to you every time.

CHAPTER 7

Fueling Your Success
Through Motivation

Want to know something many people lack? An ability to stay motivated. This probably does not surprise you. Countless people set
out goals for themselves, many people follow through with the creation of
a plan and then… nothing happens. Action will not be continued on a plan
if a person lacks motivation, and therefore many goals remain unfulfilled.

Ehsan Bayat, CEO of Afghan Wireless and the Bayat
Foundation, exemplifies the importance of motivation.
Ehsan is an Afghan American who fled from Afghanistan
to America as a teenager in 1979 during the Soviet invasion.
He put himself through school and obtained a degree in
Engineering. An ambitious entrepreneur at an early age,
Ehsan started, then owned and operated, several restaurants
and small businesses in the USA. All the while, he always
maintained the desire to one day return to Afghanistan to
help the devastated people of his country who had been at
war from both external and internal forces for decades.

In early 2002, the opportunity presented itself for him to
visit Afghanistan. There he witnessed the destruction that

had occurred throughout the past over 20 years since he'd left. Right then, the opportunity he had been waiting for to serve and assist the people of Afghanistan presented itself. Ehsan started Afghan Wireless, offering the first cell phone service in the country. The company grew to serve millions, connecting the people of Afghanistan for the first time not only with each other, but to the outside world.

He subsequently opened radio stations and TV stations. He is also building power plants to serve his people. Afghan Wireless is currently the largest employer in the entire country. Ehsan, along with his wife, Laya, founded The Bayat Foundation, built on "nourishing the lives of Afghans." The Bayat Foundation has built hospitals throughout the country and has provided clean drinking water, food, clothing and shelter to millions of Afghans. His desire to help his people has made him wealthy beyond all measures financially, but even wealthier in spirit and riches that can't be measured.

What backed him each step along the way? Motivation! Ehsan's motivation, fueled by his goal of serving the people of a devastated country, was fixed into his subconscious mind as a very young man, mixed with inner faith that he would one day achieve his dream. This resulted in his desire to act immediately when the opportunity arouse, changing the lives of millions of Afghans for the better.

Consider the most successful person you know. Do you think this person is motivated to succeed? Without a doubt, the answer is yes. Success is unattainable without the personal motivation to do so.

A while back, while watching TV with a relative, a commercial came on for a new product. Our relative exclaimed, "Hey, that was my idea first! Ask anyone—I've been talking about that idea for ages!"

What's the difference between our relative and the inventor of that product (who, by the way, went on to make millions and millions of dollars)? Motivation. While the idea may have been in our relative's head, they never *did* anything about it. They may have shared the idea excitedly with others, but they had no motivation to take any real action to create it and market it for the masses. The inventor, on the other hand, thought of the same idea, made it their goal to invent and make this product successful and followed the key steps to move it forward. What's more, they were driven by constant motivation to do such a thing. And just like that, the inventor succeeded.

That story probably isn't all that unfamiliar to you. There are plenty of people you encounter in life who have a "Why not me?" attitude. They see CEOs of Fortune 500 companies who own big homes and vacation in the most luxurious places in the world and their mind goes immediately to "Why not me.?" Here's the truth—it *can* be them. It can be *you*. But persistent motivation must be behind your plan to get there… otherwise, it just isn't going to happen.

"The only man who never makes a mistake is the man who never does anything."
—Theodore Roosevelt[37]

As you know now, it's a whole lot easier to give the bare minimum, and that's what plenty of people do. Instead of doing more than is expected of them (which we know is vital to success) they do whatever they need to do, and nothing more. These people are generally not the motivated type.

"Initiative is to success what a lighted match is to a candle."
—Orlando Aloysius Battista[38]

Motivation is the fuel that ignites success. You can have a positive mindset, a goal, a plan, inner faith and a habit of doing more than is expected of you, but without motivation, you will go nowhere. You will reach a road bump and it will be enough for you to give up.

Those who are motivated are action takers. They are always looking to progress forward, no matter what hurdles may stand in their way. If they're unable to solve the problem on their own, they find someone who can help them solve it. Because of this, ideas that may have originally seemed impossible are now as possible as could be. Goals are achieved time and time again.

Motivated people have a positive mindset toward their goal all the time. They feel good about what they're trying to achieve. Procrastination is not even a concept in a motivated person's mind because they're action-oriented. As we've learned, there is a clear difference between someone who is willing to do the job at hand and someone who wants to go above and beyond to get things accomplished. The latter person is fueled by motivation toward the achievement of what they want in life.

Alberto Gonzales was the United States' first Hispanic Attorney General—and he worked his way there from the bottom up fueled by personal motivation. He was raised in Houston, TX by Mexican migrant workers who spoke very little English. After finishing high school, he joined the U.S. Air Force and took classes with the U.S. Air Force Academy. Wanting to continue furthering his education, he went on to get his bachelor's degree from Rice University and then his law degree from Harvard University before working at a law firm in his home state practicing business law.

He continued to work hard at his practice and ultimately became the legal counsel for George W. Bush, Texas Governor at the time, before then becoming Texas Secretary of State and then a justice on the Texas Supreme Court.

When Bush became president, Gonzales joined him in Washington, D.C. as a White House counsel before working his way up to the coveted Attorney General role. His story shows the importance of ongoing motivation in achieving success of any kind—in his case being the first of his heritage to obtain a prominent U.S. government role.[39]

A key apart of motivation is being persistent. How many times have you started a new year with a list of resolutions for yourself, only to give up on all of them within a couple of weeks? It's quite common for this to happen. If you're not adequately motivated—and persistent at every turn—there is just no way you will be able to keep up with anything you're trying to achieve, no matter how big or small. This is why we emphasized earlier that you need to establish a goal that makes you feel good. The goal provides you with the foundation for your motivation and makes it something you *want* to do, as opposed to something that you *have* to do. Likewise, it further helps you to keep your eye on the prize and not just give up when you hit a hurdle.

> *"Obstacles are those frightful things you see when you take your eyes off your goal."*
> *—Henry Ford*[40]

Achieving your goal, for example, will require much persistence and self-discipline. It will be far easier to give up than it will be to remain motivated and complete tasks along the way. Let's say your goal is a personal one, such as to lose weight. Let's say you'd like to lose 30 pounds in the next 3 months. Your plan includes working out 4–5 times per week and following a healthy diet plan. On a cold winter's night when you're exhausted from a long day of work and supposed to be going to the gym and cooking yourself a healthy dinner, wouldn't it be a whole lot easier to go home, change into sweatpants and order a pizza? Of course! But with the right motivation—you will be able to stick to your intended plan. Without it, the odds of achieving your goal are incredibly minimal.

Successful people know the importance of using motivation to focus on one or a couple of goals at a time, rather than drowning themselves in many conflicting goals. Let's go back to the idea of New Year's resolutions for a moment. Have you ever started a new year with a laundry list of resolutions? More likely than not, you failed on all of these resolutions, right? It becomes incredibly overwhelming to focus on so many goals at once, and often wears people out (and, you guessed it, decreases their level of motivation). Before they know it, they're throwing their hands in the air and saying, "Forget about it, I'm done trying!" If this seems all too familiar, next year keep your list to only one or two items, maximum. Focus in wholly on them. You'll immediately find your motivation is increased from previous years.

Motivation is heavily connected back to the concept of building your inner faith as well. Without faith in yourself that anything is possible, it will be hard to find the needed motivation.

Motivation leads to follow-through on your part, plain and simple. Even the very best idea, set as someone's goal, with the best possible plan in place and all other key factors aligned cannot be successful if you do not have motivation. Motivation is the element that drives you forward each day to achieve your goal. Without it, the ship will sink.

"There are two types of people who never amount to anything. There are those who never do anything except what they are told to do. And there are those who cannot even do what they are told to do. The people who get ahead do the things that

should be done without being told. And they don't stop there.
They go the extra mile and do much more than is expected
of them."
　　　—Andrew Carnegie[41]

Your imagination can help build your motivation, because as you'll recall, you can achieve anything you can conceive. This brings us right back to our teachings on positive mindset. If you're able to visualize something in a positive way, you're able to achieve it. Using your sense of imagination will allow your mind to open to more possibilities and ways to achieve your goal(s) that you otherwise may have not even considered. Imagine the best possible situation for yourself—personally, professionally and academically. You feel excited, right? That excitement is motivation!

Likely you've heard of a vision board. Often vision boards are helpful in getting and keeping people motivated during their journey to achieve their goal. As you now know, positive thoughts and visions result in positive outcomes when backed by action. A vision board takes those positive visions you have about the things you want in life and puts them onto a physical board that you can look at and be motivated by. Vision boards can be as simple as a poster board covered in magazine cut outs of the things you want out of life: a beautiful home, a nice car, money, a family, a particular vacation spot, optimum health, and so on.

Here's something important to remember when you're creating one, however. Make sure everything you put on the vision board makes you *feel* good as well. Just as you know right away if a thought or a vision in your head makes you feel good or bad, a physical representation of something you want will elicit the same type of response. So, if going to a baseball game for your favorite team makes you feel good, you might consider adding a picture of a baseball game to your vision board as well. This doesn't mean you're trying to become a baseball player as part of your goal, but rather will serve as a reminder of how you want to feel along your personal journey to achieve whatever it is that you want.

A vision board, which can be kept in a prominent place in your home or office for instance, will not only guide your thoughts and visions in the right way regularly, it will also serve as a constant motivator to get you where you want to be because you'll be looking at it all the time. If it becomes something that no longer provides motivation, take things off it and put up new visions. It's as simple as that.

Sparking constant motivation at every moment on your path to achieve your goal can feel unrealistic, but it doesn't have to be. In addition to the creation of a vision board, here are some other easy tactics you may consider implementing in order to foster motivation or to bring back motivation when you feel you've lost it along the way:

Set Up a Personal Rewards System

Rewards are motivators, there is no doubt about it. Look back on the plan you've established to reach your goal and see if there are key milestone points that might be worthy of a personal reward. Rewards can be either small or big, whatever works best for you.

A great example we've heard is that when a big accomplishment is made, take yourself out to a fancy dinner. Treating yourself to a special meal in itself may act as a form of congratulations to yourself, and encouragement to keep going. It's worked for many people we know!

Use the Power of Like-Minded People Around You

In a later chapter, we will discuss surrounding yourself with the right people. Those people should have your back and vice versa. If you feel like you're losing steam on your goal and plan to achieve it, reach out to one of these close, like-minded people. Explain why you're feeling this way and ask for their help to bring back the motivation you need. Then, reciprocate the favor should they find themselves unmotivated down the road.

Re-evaluate Those Around You

Pay attention closely—are the people you've surrounded yourself with naysayers, always offering up reason after reason why your goal can't be achieved? It's quite possible the people you've been surrounding yourself with are bringing your motivation level down without you even realizing it. If you're feeling unmotivated and finding this to be the case, it's certainly OK to separate yourself from these people for a period of time to the best of your ability. Instead, focus on what the positive forces around you have to say. They're bound to bring you up—and the effects will be almost immediate.

Stick to Your Deadlines

This one is so important because those who tend to miss their deadlines again and again will slowly but surely become procrastinators. And procrastination is an enemy of motivation. By establishing and sticking to your deadlines, you'll continue to wow yourself with how much you're able to personally accomplish in a tight timeframe.

Use Your Favorite Songs to Your Advantage

You know how listening to your favorite songs can always make you feel happy? Use this to your advantage when it comes to motivation. Pick a few of your favorites and begin to mentally associate them with success. Every time you hear them, picture that you've achieved all it is you want to achieve. Do this until it becomes a habit. You'll soon find that when you listen to the songs, your mind is—without hesitation—taken to a place of motivation to achieve your goals. It will get you fired up!

Self-help guru Tony Robbins—among many others—refers to this as "anchoring." Essentially, what you're doing with this exercise is creating an association between two things in your mind that may otherwise not have anything to do with each other, and connecting them for a good purpose. The stronger the emotion you're connecting, the stronger it will work.

Refer Back to Your Favorite Part of This Book (Or Another Inspirational Passage)

Find a passage—either in this book or elsewhere—that brings you inspiration. Highlight it. Then, come back to it often. If you feel like your mind has been taken off course, re-read the passage again. It will serve to ground you and bring your mind back to a motivated state.

Talk to Someone Who is Already Successful

Who better to motivate you than someone who has already found great success in their life? One simple conversation with someone you know who you consider successful (by whatever means you measure success) can change your entire sense of motivation immediately. Ask them to explain their journey to success. Ask them how they remained motivated. Ask them what they're working to achieve now in their life and how they're feeling about the progress. Hearing what they have to say will excite something inside of you.

Change Your Computer or Phone Background

Just as your vision board can motivate you greatly, a simple image on the background of your computer or cell phone screen can do just the same. Think of what image you'd associate with either success and/or inspiration in regard to your goal. Then, make that image your background. You'll unintentionally be looking at this image of inspiration countless times in a given day, subconsciously building up your motivation to achieve success.

Motivation encourages people to act right away. When was the last time you were really excited about a new goal for yourself? Think of how it felt in that moment when you first decided you were going to plan to achieve it. The quicker you moved on it, the more of that initial excitement and enthusiasm there was pumping through your veins, right? (On that point, in our chapter on goal setting and planning we discussed the fact that, without a proper plan to achieve a goal, it will be impossible to achieve it. Remember, though, that we also made a point there to mention that plans can change along the way. While you'll certainly want a plan in place, as you're embarking on your journey to success, you'll also want to use that motivation you have to launch your initiative quickly. Don't get caught up in the specifics of your plan such that it prevents you from ever actually taking action on it.)

Motivation will encourage each of us to take chances. As you can imagine, the ability to take chances, yet again, separates those who are successful from those who are not. It separates those who are able to achieve their wildest dreams from those who only receive minimum returns.

A wonderful thing about motivation is that it can take you above and beyond any success you could have ever initially dreamed of. Motivation can open doors for you that you never even realized were there. Motivation prevents you from settling for anything less than what you desire and deserve out of life.

"Desire is the key to motivation, but it's determination and commitment to an unrelenting pursuit of your goal—a commitment to excellence—that will enable you to attain the success you seek."
—Mario Andretti[42]

CHAPTER 8

Sparking Ongoing Enthusiasm

At the start of any path to success, whether personal, professional or academic, you're naturally going to feel a sense of enthusiasm (and if you don't, you should certainly reconsider what you're aiming to achieve!). You'll have a clear vision of where you want to be and it will make you feel good and excited at the thought of getting there. The beginning is the easy part, as we all know. Getting there is where things get difficult. Throughout your path to success, there may be times when you feel like your enthusiasm is lacking. Enthusiasm, just like motivation, is critical to pushing your plan forward and overcoming any hurdles that pop up along the way.

The topic of enthusiasm draws many similarities to what we just learned about motivation. If you're not enthusiastic about achieving your goal, you will not be motivated to do so. You will be like a car attempting to run without gas. Tasks will seem daunting instead of stimulating. With a lack of enthusiasm, reaching your goal will seemingly take forever, as you'll find yourself pushing off tasks instead of jumping in and accomplishing them.

Let's take a moment here to revisit where we currently are with your journey to success:

- You've been clear with yourself about what happiness means to you, personally.

- You've learned how to overcome your limiting beliefs.
- You've created a positive mindset for yourself.
- You've defined your goal and your plan to achieve it.
- You've worked on building up your inner faith.
- You've started to practice the habit of doing more than is expected of you in situations.
- You've wrapped your head around the importance of motivation in being successful.

What you may have not realized is that, along the way so far, you've been naturally building up your enthusiasm. Every time you stop and think about your goal and how you'll get there, something inside of you is sparking with enthusiasm. Every time you spend a few minutes visualizing yourself having achieved your goal, that enthusiasm sparks even brighter. All the things we've worked on so far are developing your enthusiasm more and more. And it will continue to grow from here, as long as you refuse to let any hurdles dampen the fire.

It's human nature to feel a sense of defeat when things aren't working out as you may have planned. Remember, we have complete control over our own thoughts… *complete and total control!* This means that when something pops up that stands in our way of achieving our goal, we can immediately dismiss any thought of failure and instead evaluate a way around it.

Look at your plan again—are there areas that can change should a hurdle arise? Without a doubt the answer to that will be yes. There is always a solution. If you're not seeing a way, look longer and harder. Sleep on it. Wake up with enthusiasm and look at the plan with fresh eyes. Don't be afraid to ask for help. You've been helping others along the way—it may be the perfect time to receive those returns we talked about.

That's another big difference between successful people and those who are not—their willingness to be persistent. Successful people never let a day pass without doing something to move their plan forward, despite any hurdles in their way. They'll try and try again until they get the result they want. And you know what's building up as they go? That's right—enthusiasm. Every time you take a step toward achieving your goal, no matter how big or little it may be, what you're really doing is reminding yourself that you will achieve your goal, no matter what, and no matter how long it takes. Your internal enthusiasm is blazing.

> *"I will persist until I succeed. I will try, and try, and try again."*
> *—Og Mandino*[43]

The power of your mind can help you to maintain enthusiasm every step of the way. Enthusiasm requires mental control, just as maintaining a positive mindset requires control. Similar to how we've trained our thoughts and actions to be positive, we can train ourselves to have constant enthusiasm and to be a "high energy" person, especially when it comes to getting what we want.

Right now, you may be thinking, "How is that possible? How can I really remain enthusiastic most of the time?" The thing is, you can. We promise you that. And maintaining that enthusiasm as it pertains to achieving your goal will only prove to enhance your ability to succeed.

Here's a great example of enthusiasm at a very high level. This person has not only been able to maintain his personal enthusiasm, but has made it contagious to everyone around him.

> *The enthusiasm displayed by Tom Brady, quarterback of the New England Patriots has taken him and his team to unprecedented levels of success in professional football. As*

of the writing of this book, he and the Patriots have won six Super Bowls and have appeared in nine super bowls over the past 17 years. [44] For those of you who are not familiar with the NFL, there are 32 teams competing each year for the Super Bowl and the simple fact that one of those teams has made it more than 50 percent of the time in the past 17 years is remarkable.

And it's not just that the Patriots have had a well-performing team—Brady is the only player that has been on the team for all of these Super Bowl appearances. His enthusiasm both on and off the field is contagious with his teammates and his fans and further displays his leadership skills.

Brady's unwavering enthusiasm has not only made him one of the most noteworthy football players ever to play the game, but has set the bar higher for all athletes on an international level. He has set a new level of excellence in the sporting world and also a level of expectation beyond what was even dreamed possible. His enthusiasm for what he does has him playing the sport into his 40s (well past that of a typical NFL player) with no end in sight.[44]

You can train your mind to be habitually enthusiastic by telling it to be so. You might even consider saying these words to yourself aloud a few times each day: "I am excited to achieve my goal and I know, without a doubt, that I will be able to achieve it."

Being enthusiastic makes the process of moving toward your goal more enjoyable and fun.

Here's a simple trick: You might consider keeping a list of all the times you've felt an overwhelming sense of enthusiasm along your path to achieve your goal. Detail every aspect of how you felt in that moment, what triggered it, and any other details you feel may be important. When enthusiasm is lagging, revisit the list. Read it in its entirety. It will remind you of how you should be feeling.

An important part of maintaining enthusiasm is fighting off thoughts that might trigger fear, jealously, revenge, doubt and greed. You have a lot of work to be done ahead of you, you simply don't have the extra time for those negative emotions. Be mindful of when such thoughts creep into your mind. Dismiss them. And do so right away.

If you feel your enthusiasm is slipping mentally, it's a good practice to try to translate enthusiasm into physical action. Walk into the next room you're entering with all the confidence in the world. Smile and shake hands firmly. Show excitement when listening to whoever you're speaking to and respond in an equally excited tone of voice. Surely you've heard the saying, "Fake it 'til you make it." Let's apply that here. While you don't want to come off as phony, it's OK to force this enthusiasm if it's not coming naturally. You'll notice quickly how even the most boring of conversations will have a sense of excitement now. You can never be sure you're the smartest person in the room or the most skilled, but you can use your own control to ensure you're the most enthusiastic person in the room.

Plus, enthusiasm is contagious. Others can spread it to you as easily as you can spread it to them. It will draw people to you. All the while, what's happening inside your mind? You're training your brain to be habitually enthusiastic.

Being enthusiastic will pay off for you, always. Think of enthusiasm as you would any other thought or action you put out into the world. If you put out positive, enthusiastic thoughts and actions, you will receive positive returns every time. If you put out negative, apathetic thoughts and actions, you will receive negative (or a lack of any) returns as a response. Again, this is tried and true. It is applicable each and every time.

*"A mediocre idea that generates enthusiasm will go further
than a great idea that inspires no one."*
—*Mary Kay Ash*[45]

Enthusiasm translates to action on your goal. It's taking what you believe
you can achieve and making it actually happen. Without enthusiasm, nothing would get done. And while most people have that initial enthusiasm to
achieve their goals, very few will be able to properly maintain it.

Enthusiasm allows people to see opportunities in places they wouldn't
have before. Maintaining ongoing enthusiasm will allow people to view
situations completely differently. They'll focus on the things they can do
something about versus the things they can't do something about. They'll
be more effective in their work toward their goal.

Start being enthusiastic about everything and do it over and over again.
Keep at it until it begins to come more and more naturally to you. Along
the way, apply that enthusiasm to your goal and in each step of your plan
to get there. In every interaction you participate in, be enthusiastic.

*"There is real magic in enthusiasm. It spells the difference
between mediocrity and accomplishment."*
—*Dr. Norman Vincent Peale*[46]

Enthusiasm can be maintained by keeping your eyes on the prize.
Imagine yourself having succeeded. Bring that vision board you created
to a more prominent place in your home or office. Use it to conjure up
positive feelings and to reignite your enthusiasm, and in turn motivation,
to achieve your goal.

Here is another exercise you may consider trying: Take a few minutes
in the morning in front of a mirror and talk out loud to yourself in the most
enthusiastic way possible about your goal and your plan to achieve it. You
may consider enthusiastically talking about how happy you are feeling as

you pursue it and how you will feel once you've achieved it. It may feel a bit awkward to do at first, but after some practice, it will not only prove to further your positive mindset, build your inner faith, and enhance your enthusiasm for your goal, it is also a sure way to set your day as a whole in the right direction.

The benefits of remaining enthusiastic throughout your path to success are endless. For one, if you're someone who is constantly enthusiastic, you know what that means… you're constantly happy! The time spent working on your plan to achieving your goal will, in many cases, be a lot longer than the time spent celebrating its eventual achievement. Having enthusiasm along the way to achieving your goal means you'll have felt happiness all the time, not just once you've accomplished your goal. Remember, it would be a long, gloomy life if we were *only* happy at the moment we've achieved our goals, right?

The benefits of being enthusiastic go on. Over time, by learning to maintain and control your enthusiasm, you will experience an increased sense of imagination as well as an increased belief that anything is possible. Enthusiasm will benefit you every step of the way because it will take tasks that may otherwise have seemed boring and make them exciting for you to complete. Enthusiasm not only makes a goal seem attainable; it also fosters your own self-confidence.

Have to rely on others to achieve your goal? Maintaining enthusiasm will make it easier to sell yourself. It will make it easier to make those key connections with people because they'll be drawn to you.

> *"Enthusiasm is the mother of effort, and without it nothing great was ever achieved."*
> *—Ralph Waldo Emerson*[47]

We think it's quite important to close our chapter on enthusiasm with this note: If you are constantly faced with a lack of enthusiasm as it pertains to achieving your goal—for months and possibly years on end—this may be a clear sign to you that something is not right with the goal itself. Perhaps the goal you've set out for yourself really isn't the right one for you. Perhaps it was really a goal someone else wanted you to achieve, rather than one you wanted to achieve on your own. Is there something else you'd like to achieve that perhaps you are more suited for? While you shouldn't give up on your goal because of obstacles you face in your plan, you should certainly reevaluate it if the idea of achieving the goal is not making you *feel good*. Remember that living a successful life is directly connected to living a happy life, and while goals and definitions of success and happiness vary greatly from person to person, the core concept there remains the same. It's vital to remember that and set out goals and plans accordingly.

CHAPTER 9

Taking Control of Your Life Through Self-Discipline

T hroughout this book, so far, there has been an underlining message, and it's an incredibly important one to remember: Each of us has complete and total control over whether we are successful or not. This is because we can fully control our thoughts, no matter what. We can make it so that every thought we have, and thus every action we take, is a positive and productive one, and that—in cases where negative situations do arise—our mind is trained to look at what the benefit in it would be. Controlling our thoughts and actions in such a way is the foundation of what will make each of us able to succeed. We have control to tell ourselves and the universe that success is the absolute *only option.*

> *"Maintaining the right attitude is easier than regaining the right attitude."*
> *—Unknown*

When we're able to control our minds as we've been practicing, we're showing self-discipline. When we're not, we're showing a lack of self-discipline. It's as simple as that. Self-discipline is necessary if we want to achieve success of any kind. We need to set the appropriate rules and boundaries for ourselves (depending on what our goal is) and use self-discipline to make sure they're followed. Without self-discipline, no man or woman would ever be able to achieve success. Without self-discipline, positive and negative thoughts would both flow freely and effortlessly in our minds.

Self-discipline allows you to take control over not only your thoughts, but your emotions as well. Naturally, some of the emotions we have are positive emotions. These may be emotions of happiness, enthusiasm and hope. Other emotions are negative, and include emotions like sadness, fear and jealousy.

We should note here that even positive emotions can turn negative if not controlled through self-discipline. Just as you should not lose control of your thoughts, you cannot let emotions run wild or out of control as you're working toward your goal. You must execute your power to control emotions however possible.

If you're someone who has trouble with this concept, the trick is to be extraordinarily mindful of the emotions you're having and not allow your emotions to control *you*. If you're feeling the emotion of fear come up, stop it in its tracks and counteract it. Let's say that fear is stemming from the fact that you are scared you're never going to be able to meet your goal's initial deadline. First, you should remind yourself that the more time you spend fearful of not achieving your goal on time, the less time you actually have to achieve it. Think of your negative emotions as wasted time as it pertains to reaching your goal. In this particular situation, you might try counteracting that fear with enthusiasm. Use a day planner to specify in detail how you'll manage your time in the next two or three weeks to get to where you'd like to be with your plan. In this scenario, you'll have used your self-discipline to both control your emotions and get you into action mode.

A person who shows great self-discipline in situations is the one who takes times to think before they act on something. While fast decision-making is an incredibly important attribute in successful people, it's also—of course—very important to mentally consider the pros and cons of an action or decision rather than simply making it on a whim. Self-discipline in this process calls on a person to balance their emotions with reason. Having trained ourselves to be hyper-aware of our emotions we're already halfway there. Evaluating the situation logically and rationally is that key second component. Bear in mind that certain decisions will be more driven by your emotions than by reasoning, and vice versa. However, generally speaking, you should aim to strike a balance between the two.

Please note that most people make decisions based *strictly* on their emotions (how that decision will make them *feel*), then back the decision up with their own logic behind it. You however, will look to blend both your emotions and logic to come to decisions and take actions. And, it's done through self-discipline

In essence, self-discipline describes our willpower. If you have the will to control your thoughts and actions—and the will to succeed—you're setting yourself up to achieve much more than others around you who lack that self-discipline. The very special thing about self-discipline is that it allows us to look at a situation, and mentally drive it in our own favor, no matter what. Think of the biggest hurdle you can imagine coming your way on your path to achieve your goal. Imagine that imaginary hurdle becomes a reality. While those who lack self-discipline to control the situation may let this hurdle stop them completely, those with self-discipline will mentally find a positive in the adversity, and will have the will to take action on it to overcome that hurdle.

> *"It's easy to have faith in yourself and have discipline when you're a winner, when you're number one. What you've got to have is faith and discipline when you're not a winner."*
> *—Vince Lombardi*[48]

Showing self-discipline is not always easy. We know that. In fact, it's far easier to just let things happen as they may without exerting any willpower to guide them in one direction or another. But living in a such a way means that you're allowing outside forces to completely dictate what it is that happens to you and the outcome of your goal. You're giving those outside forces the complete power, and so everything that happens will be that of chance. Sure, things may turn out good. But they may also turn out bad. Wouldn't you rather be the one controlling how situations turn out? You have the power to do so!

Using self-discipline can ensure you maintain a positive mindset. It can serve as the force that will help you to attract what you want and repel what you don't want.

You might be tempted to sleep in on a Saturday morning after a long week of work. Self-discipline will drive you to get up out of bed early and instead use that time to put in work toward your goal. Self-discipline also comes into play when it comes to time management. In today's day and age particularly, a lot of time is wasted on things such as scrolling through social media channels and watching Netflix. While it's nice to take a mental break to partake in those activities now and then, consider how much more productive you will be toward the achievement of your goal if you are able to use self-discipline to remove yourself from those distractors and focus on completing necessary tasks that will move you toward success.

"By constant self-discipline and self-control you can develop greatness of character."
—Grenville Kleiser[49]

Managing your time can be as simple as keeping a detailed day planner, as we've previously mentioned. Not only can the day planner help to keep you organized on what tasks need to be completed by certain deadlines, it can also help you specify exactly how much time you plan to spend on each task. It will keep you on track and help you to ensure you're using your time most productively.

If you're someone who thinks you lack self-discipline in this area and feel you're wasting a lot of time on menial things, try this time auditing exercise: For three days, write down everything you do while you are awake and how long you are doing said activity for. This should even include things like "Went to lunch with a coworker for one hour," "Cleaned the kitchen after dinner for 30 minutes," and "Scrolled through Instagram for 30 minutes before bed." Some of the things on your list will be things you must do in a given day (i.e., brushing your teeth, cooking meals, etc.), but it's likely you'll find some areas that you can cut back on in order to free up more time to focus on your goal. After three days, closely evaluate that list for activities that you deem as wasted time. Then, this is where your self-discipline comes into play… make sure you begin to slice back on those areas of wasted time in upcoming days and use that time instead to work on your goal.

Be realistic with yourself that there will always be temptations that come in and try to pull you away. However, if you've worked up your self-discipline enough and remain focused, those distractions won't be successful in pulling you away from your goal.

A test of your self-discipline may appear when opportunities to jump ship on your goal arise. Self-discipline will keep you on course for what it is that you really wanted to achieve.

Consider this example. A world-renowned basketball player practiced the art of self-discipline beyond that of any athlete. He led his team, the Chicago Bulls, to 6 NBA championships in the 1990's. He had incredible, natural talent, but then again, so do many others. What separated him from everyone else was the self-discipline he had regarding practicing and working out to keep improving his game and his stamina. He was so dedicated to being the best that he practiced every single day for most of his professional career—even days when he was exhausted from already playing a game. This man was Michael Jordan. He was the best in the game, but he didn't sit back satisfied with where he was. Instead, even in a physically exhausted state, he had the self-discipline to work at making himself even better.[50]

Just as our thoughts, actions and emotions can be managed through self-discipline, so can our ego. Our ego must be controlled during our path to success, as our egos say a lot to the people around us about who we are. If your ego is lacking, it can play against you poorly. Likewise, if it's overinflated, it can make others around you feel as though you're arrogant and not want to make meaningful connections with you. There is a fine line here.

We must practice using self-discipline to protect our ego as well. Here is a technique from Dr. Napoleon Hill used to help protect one's ego. We find it incredibly useful:

"You need a technique to protect your inner self, your ego, from the damaging effects of negative ideas.

There are three walls to build around your ego. The outermost wall is just high enough to keep out people who have no business getting in to take up your time. This wall should have several doors, and if someone can establish a reasonable right to your time, let that person in. But make sure he or she establishes that right first.

The middle wall is much taller, and it has a single door you must watch closely. You should admit only a few people, the ones who have established the fact that they have something you want or something in common which will be mutually helpful.

The third and innermost wall is so tall that no one will ever scale it; it has no doors. You should not allow anyone inside that wall because it protects your ego. If you let people wander in, they will wander back out with things you cherish, leaving behind worry and anxiety. Build this wall around your ego, and make a place where you can retire by yourself and communicate with Infinite Intelligence."[51]

Self-discipline also can work in our favor by helping us to open our imagination to goals and pathways we can work toward. Using self-discipline, we can put action in to make these visions of our imagination a reality. This is unlike a simple daydream where we happen upon a lottery winning, for instance. Our self-discipline knows work and action is required if we're going to achieve great success, so it sets our mind to do so.

Consider our relative, Angie, who has used self-discipline to excel beyond measure in her career. Angie began freelance writing for Johnson & Johnson more than 20 years ago, developing some of the company's most memorable and compelling annual reports and directing important strategic communication programs. When assignments would come in, she exercised self-discipline to immediately tackle them— and do so to the very best of her ability. Giving less than 110 percent was never an option, even while she balanced her freelance position with being a single mother of two young children.

And, do you know what happened? The company took notice. They saw the value she brought to the organization and how hard she was willing to work and they brought her on full-time. Fast-forward years later and Angie continues to work as an executive at Johnson & Johnson where she is a highly-respected member of their global communication team. She has been able to fulfill her goals both professionally and personally, managing to own a gorgeous home at the Jersey Shore where she single-handedly raised her children into equally-as-successful adults.

"If you're sitting around waiting on somebody to save you, to fix you, to even help you, you are wasting your time because only you have the power to take responsibility to move your life forward."
—Oprah Winfrey[52]

Self-discipline can make it a whole lot easier for us to make meaningful connections with others, which we will get to in further detail in an upcoming chapter. This is because we can ensure what we say and do is always appropriate, such as not speaking out negatively about other people and their ideas and beliefs, and not trying to push our beliefs on others in an unwarranted manner.

"Discipline is the bridge between goals and accomplishment."
—Jim Rohn[53]

As we know, taking control over our own mind and our own actions makes it possible to succeed at anything we want in life. Embrace the fact that your self-discipline allows you to have this control, but you must exercise self-discipline for it to make an impact. Keep your mind always on the things you want out of life and never on the things you do not want, and self-discipline will guide you to succeed.

CHAPTER 10

Surrounding Yourself with the Right People

So far, our discussion of ways to live a more successful life has been heavily focused on things you personally have control over. As we all know, there are endless things in life that we do not have control over, one of the main ones being how other people behave. Where you can exercise your own personal control here is by surrounding yourself with the *right* people and, in cases where the wrong people are forced into your life, managing how you interact with them in the right way.

When it comes to living a successful (and happy!) life, having the right people—those who are positive, supportive and like-minded to us—in our company makes all the difference. In a moment, we'll dive into that further. For now, let's quickly talk about managing how you interact with those people in your life who are *not* the right people, because no matter what, some of them will be present in your life here or there.

Sometimes these people pop into your life quite briefly. Being skilled at your ability to deflect their negativity in a given moment is crucial. Consider this example of the success story of Evelyn Brooks, a Latina designer and entrepreneur.[54] On her path to success with her company Evelyn Brooks

Designs—a company that designs eco-friendly jewelry—she encountered the worst kind of negative person. She recalls encountering a potential client who rejected her, noting that they "only worked with Americans." When Evelyn replied that she was, in fact, an American citizen, the person said again, "I only work with real Americans."

Evelyn could have let this get to her, but instead she dismissed it completely, and moved on. Now her business is booming, thanks to her ability to stay focused and persistent in following her dream, despite anyone who tried to stand in her way.

Other times, a negative person is more of a regular in our lives. Think about this for a moment: Do you have a close friend, family member, coworker or the like who is just plain negative? Maybe they are constantly speaking negatively about their own life and everything in it, or maybe they're even going so far as to bring you down too.

What you may find is that some of the people in that negative category are people who are *forced* into your life as such. Maybe it's a relative you live with, for example, or a friend you've had since childhood who you are unable to ever fully cut ties with. Similarly, in addition to having those who are negative around you, it's possible you may also have people forced into your life who you just do not get along with or who pose a constant burden to you. It's OK. We all have them. The point here is not to stress out about the fact that this person is forced into your life and you can't rid yourself of them, but rather to properly exercise the power of your mind to manage how you interact with them.

Your power comes in terms of how you react to these people in your life. You, and only you, have the power over whether you let them affect you or not. As they're speaking to you, you can choose to let their negativity transfer to you, or you can choose to block it. That part is completely and totally in your control.

The good news is if you do an audit of the people who are regulars in your personal life, for the most part these are people you've *chosen* to be in your life. You'll quickly notice that those forced individuals we mentioned are few and far between.

Our personal life is just that… personal. When you meet someone, you—in most instances—get to decide whether that person is someone you want to associate with as a friend or significant other. If you are like-minded and have things in common, chances are you will initially gravitate to them. If they feel the same way, they will gravitate toward you. If neither of you are feeling that way, you likely will not gravitate toward each other.

Relationships with the right people in your life can help bring you up and push you further and further into a positive mental space. These people may even help build your inner faith and/or offer needed support when your motivation or enthusiasm is lacking. The relationships you have with the right people must be managed properly, just as it's important to know how to manage those with the wrong people.

Managing a good relationship properly means eliminating the idea of "keeping score." Good personal relationships in your life, be it friendships or romantic relationships, are best off when each person is willing to give 100 percent. Many times, people approach their good relationships with a 50/50 mentality, whereas one person gives 50 percent and the other person gives 50 percent. The problems there start to come into play when the two people involved begin thinking this way: "I did this for you, so next time you need to do that for me." That kind of approach can quickly sour a perfectly good relationship.

The difference between that approach and those who give 100 percent from each end in a good relationship is astounding. Try it for yourself and see. Pick someone in your life who you're close with and, for the next month, put the other person's interests ahead of yours every time. By approaching the relationship this way, you may likely begin to see that that other person begins to do the same for you, without even realizing. This makes for outstanding relationships!

Right now you may be thinking, "But, what if I put forth 100 percent and the other person doesn't? That will mean they're just taking advantage of me." That's fair to think. We know with certainty that we cannot, in any way, control other people's behaviors, so there is no guarantee that they will meet you by also going 100 percent. At the end of the day, at minimum giving that 100 percent to someone will (1) make you feel good (which is the whole point of any of this, right?) and (2) will be an exercise in doing more than is expected of you.

If after a while you're continuing to give 100 percent and the other person simply is not, feel free to reign it back a little and refocus that effort into another relationship in your life. Don't be upset with that person for not reciprocating. Accept that people behave how they will behave and that there is no control you can have other than how you think about and react to it.

Because you're doing more than is expected of you without worry over whether it is being returned to you... it will be returned. Perhaps this will not be the case in the relationship at hand, but rest assured a benefit will come to you.

For now, focus on those closest to you and give 100 percent to them. Go out of your way to do something for them. Invite them somewhere. Offer to help them with something without the thought of anything in return. Then, watch what happens. Once you see the results of how good you feel and how good they feel about you, you will want to continue this path for life.

We recently witnessed a young lady, Lia, who put 100 percent into her relationship with a boyfriend for several months. He did not reciprocate and the relationship wound up ending. On the surface this appeared to be a waste of her time, energy and emotions. However, within a couple of months of this break up she met a new boyfriend who adores her, goes 100 percent and treats her kindly. You see, her efforts with her last relationship did not go unrewarded. What she put out in her previous relationship, and now also in her current one, came back to her—just as the Law of Increasing Returns predicts it would.

Now that we've covered your close relationships, let's delve into surrounding yourself with the right people when it comes to pursuing a business or monetary goal. This section is specifically for those who are setting goals out for themselves that include starting their own business and/or running a business.

"Alone we can do so little; together we can do so much."
—Helen Keller[55]

With these types of endeavors, it is very difficult, if not impossible to, be successful alone. Even if a goal is small and seems achievable on your own without the skills or know-how of anyone else, at the end of the day you will always need at least one person to support you in some capacity.

Consider a painter, for example. He or she may have a goal of becoming a famed artist. Even without any help from others in the business to finish his paintings, the painter at minimum would need someone who is willing to assess the value of his or her finished work in order to build notoriety and fortune. Others will always play a role in your success, no matter what.

Sometimes those closest to you can be the perfect ones to help lead you toward success. Consider the Sauma brothers, who represent an unprecedented model of teamwork, among other success attributes. The six brothers grew up in turbulent

Lebanon in the 1970s and 1980s. As children, they watched their father import food and commodities into Lebanon. Their dad, Joseph, started with nothing and rose up to run a successful business in a hostile region during very trying times.

He and his wife Nada wanted much more for their children. As each of their boys would graduate traditional schooling, Joseph and Nada would encourage and support them in continuing on to higher education. Some went to college in Lebanon and Europe and some in America. Ultimately, at the encouragement of their parents, they each migrated to America one-by-one for better higher education and career opportunities.

Having learned much from their father, a key mentor and role model for them, the brothers decided they would follow in his footsteps in the import/export business and expand their trading globally. In particular, they saw a huge opportunity to export American food products. They began to secure complex export arrangements with a couple of international distributors to a few countries. Little by little their business grew and today their company, International American Supermarkets Corp, has over 100 distributors and does business in over 50 countries worldwide. The brothers added tremendous value to their company due to their teamwork, determination, and business savvy.

All the brothers have separate and distinct roles in their business and each executes with perfection while remaining in sync with the others. They are brothers first, then friends, then business partners. They all have respect and admiration not only for each other, but for their parents and the lessons they taught them as young men. Now many of their children are involved in the business with the hopes that one day they will take over and follow in their fathers' footsteps.

If you visit International American Supermarkets Corp. you will see that a full-size bronze statue of Joseph graces the entrance. To the right is a statue of Nada sitting on a park bench enjoying her favorite hobby—painting. These statues are daily reminders of the solid business and family foundation that continue to lead the six Sauma brothers' success and unity. The Sauma family not only exemplifies teamwork, but also the ability to get along with others and—perhaps most importantly—gratitude. The brothers constantly show gratitude for each other and for what their parents did for them. That gratitude is shown not only by the bronze statues erected in their parents' honor, but through the way they speak about them. The admiration and appreciation are unmatched.

If your goal is to start your own business, for example, you will need to begin by pinpointing people who have skills to start your business that you may not have. None of us know how to do *everything,* and that's OK. That is why, when necessary we need to tap into those who have skills we are lacking. When choosing people to assist you with your goal, they should be fully onboard with your goal and plan to achieve it. They should fully understand it and agree with it so that you're working together on the same path in harmony. Give these people a vested interest in achieving the goal, too.

Let's take, for example, Steve Jobs and Steve Wozniak—two men who came together in developing and building Apple. One fed off the other, and then over time, where they saw weakness as they were growing, they assembled more people to join them and do certain things better than they could. Together, they grew and developed one of the largest and most profitable companies in the world.

How can you begin to choose the individuals to assist you with your goal? Spend some time thoroughly considering what is needed to reach your goal that you, yourself, are unable to do alone. What skills, talents or personal support is needed? You should choose people for your "team" who have the ability to do those things.

Each member of your team should be selected for a specific purpose— because they have the ability to do what is needed. Do not choose individuals for your team simply because they are someone you're close with. Your best friend, for instance, may not have the insight or the skills needed to help with your goal of opening a clothing store in your town, but perhaps he or she can connect you with a contact they have who is looking to partner on a business. That contact's goal would directly align with yours.

Once you've identified people who have the ability to do the job necessary to help fulfill your goal, you must make sure those individuals can work in harmony with you and others on your team. You should all share the same mentality of success and an understanding of the power of positive thinking. Perhaps you are in need of a marketer for your business and find someone who has the skills, but whose behavior is unruly and causes arguments between you and the rest of the team. This would not be someone you want to continue working with, as the lack of harmony will be detrimental to achieving your goal.

What if you think someone has the right harmony with the rest of your team early on in the process, and you later learn they do not? Remove them as the process moves forward and replace with someone else who is a better fit. Ongoing harmony is most important, so changing group members is sometimes inevitable.

Your team should collectively be working together to strengthen each other's strengths, delegate weaknesses and stay focused on what it is that each of you are particularly good at. Your team's strengths allow you to collectively accomplish the goal.

> *"Talent wins games, but teamwork and intelligence win*
> *championships."*
> —*Michael Jordan*[56]

Let's talk professional goals specifically for a few minutes. If you're starting your own business, the team you initially put together is likely going to need to grow over time as the business is thriving. Essentially, you're going to need more people to work for you as things begin to pick up. For this type of goal, once you get to the point of growing your team, be mindful that all people working for you at that point do not have to have the exact same goal and work in perfect harmony as your initial team did, but they should be aware of what they are there to accomplish, and be recognized and compensated accordingly.

The Apple example we mentioned speaks to how important it is to have the right partner or team in place to start a business and keep it running. Once it's grown to be the large company it is today, it's clear that not every single one of Apple's current employees will have the same exact vision and passion for the company as that initial team did. However, all of the company's employees should be playing a part in the company's success by being held accountable for completing their specific job.

> *"The achievements of an organization are the results of the*
> *combined efforts of each individual."*
> —*Vince Lombardi*[57]

If you are someone whose goal is to start your own business, it will be important for you to know and understand this concept as your business grows and, in turn, your team grows. At that point, it will not only be important for you to ensure you're hiring the right people who can do their jobs well and be accountable, but you will also be responsible for ensuring *they* feel there is a benefit in it for them as well. Creating a good work environment where employees feel like their voice is heard and that they are benefitting in some way—whether that's through compensation, recognition and so on—is essential to success. As your team of trusted employees grows, you will be able to fully begin to work *on* your business, rather than *in it*—and can therefore, better position it to further grow and flourish.

Ultimately, your goal with pulling together a team of any kind is to find members who are able to successfully cooperate with each other. Cooperation between everyone on a team is incredibly important for the success of any team, no matter what. If a key member of your team is not being cooperative, try giving them a motive to cooperate.

> *"If everyone is moving forward together, then success takes care of itself."*
> *—Henry Ford*[58]

In general, when choosing members of your team remember to seek out people who are like-minded to you and who are positive thinkers. The more you're able to surround yourself with others who think the same, the more successful you will be in life.

> *Here is an example for you to consider when it comes to teamwork. The University of Connecticut (UConn) women's basketball team has been excelling in college basketball for over 20 years. Not only have they won a record-setting four straight NCAA Division I Championships, but they've also won 111 straight games, the longest winning streak in college basketball history.*[59]

How did they do it? Unlike professional players who remain on a team for many years, the team is constantly changing as the women graduate and new players arrive. So, what is their secret to unwavering success?

Once they join the team, they strive to stay connected to it forever. Even beyond graduation, the players will stay involved and are active in helping maintain the momentum from previous years. It is something that very much distinguishes the team from others in the league—they are a team now and into the future, and always have each other's back.

CHAPTER 11

The Art of Connecting with Others

C onnecting with others around you goes far beyond those you have close relationships with and those who may be directly helping you to achieve your goal. Every day we have an opportunity to connect with people in one capacity or another, and while many won't seemingly have anything to do with your goal, they may still play a key role in helping you to be successful. Let's talk about how you can make the most of your connections with the people you encounter—both verbally and non-verbally—in a given day in order to live the most successful life possible, personally, professionally and/or academically.

Consider our relative Dan who is a professional dog trainer. On the surface, the profession may not appear to be extremely suitable for achieving great financial success; however, for Dan it is. The great success he's achieved with his business lies strongly with his ability to interact with people in a positive way. His positive interactions with his clients results in more referrals for training than he and his staff can even handle. It's not just his clients he has a knack for interacting with, but—it's everyone. If you go out anywhere with Dan in his local area, there is always someone that knows him and is excited and happy to see him.

Why? He always has a smile on his face. He shakes hands firmly and looks people directly in the eye, showing interest in each and every one of them. He'll ask how their family is doing and how their dog is doing. He treats everyone like they're special and, because of that, people have a positive feeling when he's around. His ability to connect with others and do more than is expected of him in interactions has made him successful, not only financially but in all aspects of his life.

Let's look at how you can start to connect with people like that, too.

We've already covered in depth the importance of establishing a positive mindset in order to be successful. The art of connecting with others builds directly upon that. While in Chapter 3 we focused on gaining control over our own minds and the way we think, now we'll expand on that to make sure what we're then putting out into the world is positive as well. When we're connecting with people in a positive way, it not only makes those around us feel good about their interactions with us, it also ends up further establishing a positive mindset within ourselves. It's a win-win.

How we connect with others can be simplistically broken down into two categories: verbal communication and non-verbal communication. Verbal communication includes the things we say. Non-verbal communication is how our bodies physically react during interactions with others. When we're able to excel at both of these areas of communication, it will lead to better relationships with those around us, resulting in a simpler path to success for any goal.

Verbal Communication

"Nothing is ever lost by courtesy. It is the cheapest of pleasures, costs nothing, and conveys much."
—Erastus Wiman[60]

Just as it is in the case of our thoughts, everything we verbally say has an impact of some kind. Those around us listen to the things we say and the way we say those things and use that, in part, to come to a determination about who we are.

Some may approach this topic with the mindset of, "I don't care what other people think about me," and that is fine. If that is your thought process, you have a right to it. However, similar to the years of research that have been conducted on the previous topics we discussed—and all of the upcoming topics to be covered in this book—the ability to get along with others and be likable have proven to aid in living a successful life.

There are some very straight-forward ways of using verbal communication that can aid in achieving anything you set out to achieve. Essentially, the notion of "think before you speak" reigns true here. As we've learned, you should always try to keep your thoughts about something in a positive light, even when things might not seem particularly positive on the onset. Now, translate those positive thoughts into positive words. Afterall, your words and the way in which you say them carry a lot of weight. You should use your words and tone to uplift, encourage and inspire others, rather than demean someone or make them feel bad in any way.

Remember this: Once words leave your mouth, you are unable to take them back. In addition, the words we speak whether positive or negative, just like the thoughts that we have, send us in that corresponding direction.

Be Respectful

Think of someone you know who lacks respect when they speak to others. Likely, this isn't your favorite person to be around, right? Speaking with respect for people around you is vital if you want others to be drawn to you in the most positive way possible. Of course, you are not always going to agree with what others say, but just as you have control over the thoughts you think, you have complete and total control over the way you verbally speak to a person you disagree with. There is no reason to speak to anyone you encounter in life disrespectfully. Refrain on speaking out in ways that will offend others or minimize their worth.

Be Clear in What You're Saying

Successful people are decisive and pointed when they speak. This, in turn, exudes confidence and draws others in.

Listen, Listen, Listen

Listen to what others are saying. It can be tempting to interrupt with a thought you're having, but you will both get a lot more out of a conversation if you're able to fully absorb what they're trying to say, and then vice versa. A simple way of practicing this is by making it a point to remember the name of someone you're first getting introduced to. Many people claim they are incapable of doing this, so you will stand out in a crowd immediately if you master that skill.

Also, think of it this way: How do you feel after you're walking away from a conversation where the other person did most, if not all, of the talking? Likely not great. Oppositely, what if they mostly listened to what you had to say? You likely felt good about that person, right? You may have felt they were interested in you and what you had to say. Turn this around and be the listener, and people will have that good feeling about you.

*"You can make more friends in two months by becoming
interested in other people than you can in two years by trying
to get people interested in you."*
—*Dale Carnegie*[61]

Watch Your Tone

When you speak to others, it's not always the words you're saying, but how you're verbally saying them, that can mean a lot. Successful people use a confident (but not arrogant) tone of voice and avoid a rude or lackadaisical tone. Because their tone is so confident, any anxiousness in their tone that they'd otherwise have is gone. Those around them are likely to listen to what they say and take it as the truth. They'll also be more apt to wanting to help them with their goals as well.

Avoid Talking Negatively About Others

Time spent talking negatively about other people is time wasted. When you're having interactions with someone and they begin to talk negatively about someone else, steer them away from the topic and try to bring it back to the positive side. Speaking negatively attracts negativity. Every moment spent talking negatively about someone else is a moment that others spend negatively talking about you. When you are with friends, family or associates and they are talking negatively or gossiping about someone else, and you are participating, don't you ever wonder if they do the same about you when you're not around? If you are participating in the negative gossip, others are negatively gossiping about you.

Also, have you ever noticed when you've just spent time with a group of people who were speaking negatively about topics and other people, that you leave the conversation feeling a bit negative yourself? It's almost as if the negativity leaked onto you. In Chapter 3 on establishing a positive mindset, we talked about how avoiding negative people can better your mental state. That said, the same idea reigns true when considering the connections you're making. While not possible in every situation, try to stay away from people who are always talking negatively. When you're in a social situation, and everyone else is talking negative about someone, it's easy, just don't say anything, or if you are forced into conversation, say something good about that person and then just change the subject.

Think of talking about others negatively using this example. Consider a baseball game. On the field, there are a handful of players participating in the game. In the stands there are tens of thousands of spectators, many of whom are making judgements about how the players are doing in the game. If this game was your life, would you want to be a player or a spectator? You want to play, right? Every minute you spend spectating is a minute pulled away from your focus on your goal(s). Just as the players on the field are focused on winning the game they're playing and are not paying attention to what those in the stands are doing, when you'll be busy manifesting what it is that you really want in life, there simply won't be any time to talk negatively about what other people are doing.

Just remember the saying, "If you can't say something nice, don't say anything at all". This practice will earn you a lot of respect and confidence from others.

"A 24-year-old boy seeing out from the train's window shouted...
'Dad, look the trees are going behind!'
Dad smiled and a young couple sitting nearby, looked at the
24 year old's childish behavior with pity,
suddenly he again exclaimed...
'Dad, look the clouds are running with us!'
The couple couldn't resist and said to the old man...
'Why don't you take your son to a good doctor?'

The old man smiled and said...
'I did and we are just coming from the hospital, my son was
blind from birth, he just got his eyes today.'
Every single person on the planet has a story. Don't judge
people before you truly know them. The truth might surprise
you."
—Unknown

Avoid Jealousy

This is an extension of talking negatively, but is worth its own mention. No good can come out of jealousy, whether that be jealousy of someone else's success, business, car, home, promotion, relationship, school grades, college degree, or the like. No matter what, jealousy will ultimately only prove to bring you down. This goes for how you're speaking to and about others, and how you're thinking about them as well. Often people experience jealousy because they feel like someone else getting something good will hurt or prevent them from having it. This is simply not true, though. When a jealous thought comes into your head, you might consider stopping and thinking, "Does what this person has or is doing impact me personally in any negative way?" The large majority of the time, the answer will be no.

When you think or express jealousy for another person, it puts you into a negative mindset, plain and simple. You start thinking, and asking questions like, "How did they get that?" "Why do they deserve that?" and "Why can't I have what they have—I deserve it too!" These thoughts then become a self-fulfilling prophecy. As we think, so shall we be. You can easily reverse this pattern by being happy for people instead, and sincerely congratulating them. It's perfectly fine to even say or ask them, "Wow, I'm so happy for you, how did you do that? I'm asking because it's something that I want too and maybe you have some insight for me."

Success leaves clues. What they've been able to accomplish is there and ready for you to accomplish as well, if you choose. Successful people will be happy to tell you how they achieved success. Don't believe it? Just ask them and see.

What someone else has, or does not have, has *nothing* to do with you. Your success, or lack of it, in your life has nothing to do with what anybody else is doing, good or bad. If you want your fortunes to shift, you have to begin telling a different story in your mind, aloud and in your own actions. The bottom line of this very important topic of jealousy is to be happy for others' successes and let them know you are. It puts you in a positive mindset that will enable you to equal or exceed others' accomplishments.

Put an End to Complaining

We've all been in conversations where someone is complaining about problems they're experiencing and then someone else steps in and tries—and sometimes succeeds—in out-doing the first person's problems with their own. This includes familiar statements like, "Oh, that's nothing, you won't believe what happened to me last week". They're bringing themselves further and further into a negative space by attempting to try to have even more problems than the first person. This is highly counter-productive. At times, it seems like these individuals are actually expecting more problems to come, and sure enough, the Law of Attraction never disappoints.

> *"The goal in life is to have the least amount of problems, not the most."*
> *—Greg Rea*

We've conceptually shared this with you before: When others start to complain and tell you about their problems, put up the wall in your mind and don't let their negativity affect you or your mental attitude. Please note that we are not saying that you should avoid lending a sympathetic ear and we are not saying that you shouldn't help them with their problems if you can. What we are recommending is that you use this opportunity to verbally offer advice or help when and if you can, but don't let them into your mind so far that it affects your well-being or positive mindset in any way. Likewise, don't let them encourage you to begin verbally expressing complaints of your own.

On your end, don't complain. We all know someone who constantly complains—and likely they're someone we do not want to be around. Some of these types of people may even seem to have a black cloud over their head and they just keep drawing more and more problems to themselves. The more they complain, the more problems come into their lives. Ask yourself these two simple questions: Are you happier when you're around them? Do you look forward to seeing them? That's exactly what others will feel about you if you are a complainer.

Instead, try talking about the good things going on in your life and the life of others. When you begin to tell that different story, not one of lack and complaint, but one of happiness, success and positivity, it will not only change the way others see you, but it will also start to attract other good things, circumstances and people into your life.

When you have a problem in your life, seek out and find someone to talk with who you believe will be able to help you solve the problem, not just listen to you complain. The conversation should always be solution-focused. The question to ask them and yourself is simple: "How do I solve this problem/issue?" By remaining solution-focused and expecting an answer to that issue, it will always be there.

Face Your Problems Wisely

Another important rule of thumb to avoid verbally complaining about your problems with others is to not stack your problems. Instead, spread them out and conquer them one at a time. Some people seem to have the tendency to stack their problems one on top of the other until they begin to look up at a mountain of issues and it becomes overwhelming to them. It can become so overwhelming, in fact, that they end up just doing nothing about it.

You will find that when you break the problems you're facing down individually or spread them out, instead of looking *up* at the mountain, you can look *down* on each and begin to conquer them one at a time. Go after one issue you can solve immediately by taking some simple action, eliminate that one and then move on to the next. As you begin to get momentum, anything that comes along is easily defeated one-by-one. This will eventually become habit-forming, will lead to a more successful life and have a positive effect on everyone around you. To sum it up, if something comes into your life that you don't want, don't focus on the problem but instead on the solution, defeat it and move on with a winning/positive mindset.

Deal with any issue or problems in life as it comes up. Don't kick the can down the road by not dealing with the problem and just delaying it and hoping that it will eventually go away. Put out the fire while it's small and manageable, not when it's raging and out of control and you're forced to do something. You will find by dealing with problems immediately and taking action, you will have much greater peace of mind, as time worrying about it will be minimalized.

Another trick we have found to be useful when stuck on a problem is to enlist a close friend or family member and "trade" your problems. Explain the problem you're facing to this person and have them explain a problem they're facing to you. Then, solve each other's problem and bring back a solution. What you'll find is that solving another person's problem may be a whole lot simpler than your own, as you're taking the emotion completely out of the situation and just able to focus in on the facts to come to an answer.

Steer Away from Conversations About News, Politics and Religion

Unless your job or school-related activity is directly correlated with news, politics or religion, conversations of this nature can end up being quite contentious with peers who have differing beliefs from you. For instance, some people are simply infatuated with the news, especially when it involves politics. All they want to talk about is how bad the other political side is. Almost all of these types of conversations are negative. A very easy way for you to handle these situations is, when watching or listening to the news, or in conversation with others about it, ask yourself this question again: "Does this impact me personally in any negative way?" Most of the time you will find that the topic at hand has no effect on you. Rather than participating in negative talk about the topic, move on and don't allow it to get you down. Instead of spending time worrying about the economy at large, work on your own economy.

The same concept applies to religion. There are many different beliefs and everyone is entitled to believe whatever religion they choose to. Instead of trying to get others to take on your religious beliefs, allow them to believe in whatever they choose! It's their life. Remain focused on yours.

Non-Verbal Communication

Non-verbal communication refers to how your body behaves when you're interacting with others. Just as important as the things we speak about are our non-verbal communication skills. Let's discuss a couple of tricks to excel at these:

Manage Your Facial Expressions

One brief facial expression can manage to tell a person you're speaking with a lot about how you're feeling. For instance, a universal negative facial expression is one where you have a furrowed eyebrow and lips pressed tensely together. This tends to communicate anger, disgust or disbelief to whomever you are speaking to. Many times, we make facial expressions like that and aren't even aware we're doing it. The trick here is to try to be more mindful of it.

Managing your facial expressions—while often difficult to learn—will benefit you greatly. Likewise, the more you're able to learn and manage your own facial expressions, the better you'll become at reading the facial expressions of others. This is a trick used by countless successful individuals on their path to getting what they want.

Shake Hands with Authority

You've likely heard many times that how a person shakes hands says a lot about them. What does it convey? It's shown that a strong handshake is correlated, for one, with an increased sense of trust for a person. A strong handshake has also been shown to convey that a person is both self-motivated and confident. Upon greeting someone, try to keep your handshake as firm as possible while looking them in the eye in order to instantly, and without any words, show you are someone they want to know, help and/or work with.

Smile More

If you don't feel like there is an actual connection between your facial expressions and how you're feeling, try to smile the next time you're angry. Likely, you'll notice that your mood instantly enhances. That negative mindset will begin changing over quickly. Even more, a smile will serve as a much more attractive quality to those around you compared to a frown and make you appear more likable and easier to connect with. It will make you more approachable to others and friendly. You might even find you connect with someone with a smile alone—no words necessary.

Pay Attention to How You're Sitting

Imagine yourself for a moment giving a presentation to a room filled with people. Let's say everyone in the front row was slouching over lazily as they watched you present. Likely you probably wouldn't feel good about this, right? Maybe you'd assume they were bored and uninterested in being there. Their body language was saying a lot to you in those moments.

How you're sitting when you're in a meeting—or anywhere else with other people for that matter—is communicating something to those around you. It's important to sit up straight and face/lean forward toward those you're interacting with. This conveys absolute interest without you even having to say a word. It shows that you're engaged in the conversation, not just mentally but physically as well.

Stay as Relaxed as You Can

While you'll benefit from not being *fully* relaxed to the point of slouching in your chair, the more relaxed you're able to keep your body during interactions with others, the better the interaction as a whole. We all know someone who fidgets a lot when they're speaking to others—maybe it's a habit of tapping a pen, or shaking their leg or biting their nails. When we're interacting with that person it's possible they make us feel less relaxed because they are seemingly very unrelaxed and nervous themselves. While it may be difficult in all situations, the more we're able to reign in our fidgeting-type non-verbal habits, the more comfortable others will feel and the better others will respond to our interactions with them.

Keep Your Eyes from Darting Around

Did you know that if your eyes are darting around while you're talking to someone it can convey to that person that you're feeling insecure and looking for a way to get out of the conversation? Not a good thing, right? Maintaining consistent eye contact will not only show the person you're speaking with that you're interested in what they're saying, but also that you're committed to the conversation and not mentally seeking out an escape route.

And, Keep Squinting at a Minimum

Unless you're trying to see something in the far distance or the lighting is too low—squinting when you're interacting with someone tells them that you either dislike them or dislike something they are telling you. Either way, it's not good, especially interactions when you're trying to build a bond or properly connect with someone. Quit the squint, and you'll be happy you did!

Mahatma Gandhi, "The Father of India," was one of the greatest communicators in history. He had no money, no home and no political experience, but his ability to connect with others, both within India and on a global level, freed an entire nation without a single shot being fired.

Taking control over your verbal and non-verbal communication skills will, without a doubt, enhance your ability to be successful in life in every aspect. Just as you've gained control over your thoughts, follow the tips we've laid out and you'll quickly be able to translate this to make the most of your connections with others.

> *"The most important single ingredient in the formula of success is knowing how to get along with people."*
> *—Theodore Roosevelt*[62]

As you're continuing to monitor your verbal and non-verbal communication, you may also realize the concept we have come to call the "three strikes rule." As you're connecting with people throughout a given day, you may encounter one or more who are really seeming to push your buttons and making you want to throw in the towel on being polite. If one person is getting to you, that's fine, just let it go. If two people are getting to you, that's fine too. Let it go. However, if three people have gotten to you that day, that's strike three and the problem may actually be *your* mindset that day. When you get to strike three, try to stop and mentally reset. You'll instantly feel much better—we promise you that.

CHAPTER 12

Fact vs. Opinion: Weeding Through Information

"Don't base your decisions on the advice of those who don't have to deal with the results."
—Anonymous

It is likely that today alone you will participate in at least one conversation in which you are presented with someone else's opinion on a given topic. Others' opinions are shared regularly with us throughout our lives, in verbal conversations with those we encounter as well as in mass quantities online through vehicles like news articles and social media channels. If we listen closely enough, advice and opinions from others are everywhere around us at all times. People want to offer their thoughts and advice, and it's our job to determine whether what they're offering up is worthy to utilize, and whether it is fact or not. How much we let others' opinions affect our personal success is based on one thing and one thing alone…. You guessed it: The power of our mind.

In this chapter, we'll discuss how to use the power of your mind to help you determine who you should be seeking information and advice from and how to best determine whether what they're telling you is fact or opinion. Most importantly, we'll discuss how to determine whether or not information is applicable to your achievement of success.

Right now, you may be wondering, "Why is this topic important in my path to success?" Everyone is entitled to their own opinions, of course, so how could others' opinions possibly have a negative effect on us? While others' opinions on their own may not pose a threat to your path to success, an inability to weigh their opinions from fact may do so. Likewise, a tendency to seek advice from those who are not experts can cause issues all the same.

It can be quite easy to consider a statement someone has told us as fact, especially if the topic is something we feel we personally know little about. However, to be successful, we must always be certain to analyze what a person is telling us in order to come to a conclusion about whether it is actually fact or not. Consider how ineffective our plan for achieving our goal would be if we are using others' opinions as truths, rather than fully determining their validity. It could be catastrophic for our plan and could pose endless setbacks for us along the way.

Let's consider an example of a statement that can easily be considered opinion. Imagine yourself scrolling through Facebook and seeing a Facebook user comment on a picture of a dog. The comment states, "Dogs are not good pets to have. Cats are the only way to go!" While this statement wasn't necessarily positioned as an opinion, you know it to be opinion versus fact. It is common sense.

Other times, however, we can easily be deceived, and this is why it's so crucial to use the power of our minds to stop us in our tracks and remind us to question the validity of what is being said (especially when it's relevant to our goal, which we'll soon expand on). Let's say you're back on Facebook and scrolling through your feed, and you pass an article from a seemingly credible source on why walking for 30 minutes every day will lead to better overall health. A commenter writes, "You should actually walk one hour per day for optimum health." You click on the commenter's page and see he or she is a personal trainer. While this person can certainly be initially perceived as an expert on the topic with that credential, have they offered any evidence there that one hour per day of walking is better than 30 minutes per day of walking? This is where things can get tricky. Is her comment a fact or an opinion? Because it's difficult to determine on the surface, it is something that would be worth researching further if, and only if, you're someone who plans to start walking every day as a means of improving your health. If not, just disregard the temporary distraction and move on.

Opinions are thrown around as facts constantly, and it's our responsibility to train ourselves to do the necessary work to first determine if it's applicable to what we want in life, and then if so, to fully weigh fact from opinion. Being skeptical of everything everyone says all of the time can prove to be a waste of time, and, surely we also want to be trustworthy of others where possible. However, it's crucial to not let yourself be easily influenced by people at every turn without verifying both the source and their statements.

It is equally important when being presented with a negative opinion that you not let it enter your mind (we talked in an earlier chapter about putting up the walls in your mind) or affect your life and goals in anyway.

"The only opinion about your dream that really counts is yours. The negative comments of others merely reflect their limitations—not yours."
—Cynthia Kersey[63]

Most facts and opinions that we hear in a given day are unimportant and should be treated as such. The only ones that you should be concerned about are those that are applicable to your schooling, your job, your goal or anything else that is particularly important to you in your life. Everything else can simply be discarded from your mind.

When you are in conversation with someone who is providing you information on a subject, the first question you should ask yourself is, "Is this information applicable to my life/purpose?" If the answer is no, then no need to even think about it or discuss it with them any further. If it is something applicable to your life, a very easy way to determine if it is a fact, or just their opinion, is to simply ask them, "How do you know?"

You may easily be able to tell by the answer they give whether it's fact, hearsay or their opinion.

As you move forward with your plan for achieving your goal, you're going to need expert advice, no matter what. Choosing the right people to take advice from—and weighing their advice as either fact or opinion—can truly make or break your success rate. Just as we've trained our thoughts in various ways so far, we can train our minds to stop and thoroughly consider facts and opinions, especially those relevant to our goal.

Before we get into too much detail, we should stop here again and note that most of the facts and opinions we hear throughout a given day are not relevant to our life or goal. We cannot stress this point enough, because you need not clutter your mind with these unimportant things. That does not mean these statements are not important in every case, but for the purposes of achieving your goal, it is not significant that you spend any time scrutinizing such irrelevant statements. The Facebook comment about dogs versus cats that we just spoke of is a great example. The statement was simply a comment that does not need to take up, and should not take up, any of your time or energy. If your goal is relevant to health however, the second example we discussed about walking every day may very well be one you'd want to spend more time looking into and verifying. It's worthy of your time.

It's up to each of us to use our best discretion to determine which facts and opinions are worth spending time on. Once we've made such determination, we can begin exercising our "fact versus opinion" muscle by first vowing to never accept something as fact, or accepting another person as an expert, until we've done our due diligence. We can use our sense of reasoning in all relevant situations to help us decide whether something is fact or opinion. Many times, it's as simple as just slowing down for a moment, or again asking them, "How do you know?"

Often we may find ourselves moving so quickly through life that when we're listening to other people, we are not *actually* listening to what they say. If you're someone who has a very busy life, when was the last time you were able to just sit and think your own thoughts, let alone fully think through the thoughts someone else shared with you? If we pause and listen closely, it's a key step to determining whether they're being factual. Next time you're being given advice about something related to your goal, listen closely: Does this person have a motive at all in what they're telling you? Are they trying to sell you something that you may not otherwise need? Are they backing up their statements with evidence and/or examples of real-life experience? Are they being slanderous in any way?

All of those are worthy questions to be asking yourself. If you're not asking yourself those questions regularly in your conversations with others than what you're unknowingly doing is letting others around you do your thinking for you. Along your path to success and as you seek advice from those who know more on topics than you do, you must stop along the way and fact check. Don't allow someone else's thoughts to become your own without doing that due diligence. Gather the facts and do your own thinking.

> *"A wise man makes his own decisions. An ignorant man follows public opinion."*
> *—Chinese Proverb*[64]

We can consider this simple example again of someone whose goal is to lose weight. Let's say this person has set out to lose a certain number of pounds in a certain timeframe. Their plan to achieve their weight loss goal is based on one specific article they read online regarding a diet and exercise plan, and they failed to do their due diligence to make sure the diet and exercise plan outlined in the article was factual or, importantly, sustainable for long term maintenance of their goal weight. What would happen? Likely, a lot of hard work without the results they were truly hoping for, right? This shows how it can be irresponsible to rely on just one source when aiming to achieve a goal. The results of doing so can be very frustrating.

When it comes to the "expert" at hand, simply put, would you take medical advice from a lawyer? Would you take marriage advice from someone who has multiple failed marriages? Would you take swimming lessons from someone who doesn't know how to swim? Many times, it's as logical as that. Pay attention to who is speaking to you, just as much as you're paying attention to the words they are saying.

By far your best bet when seeking advice from others is to talk with someone who has already accomplished something on the subject you are interested in/desire. If it's weight loss, speak to someone who has succeeded in losing weight and maintaining it. If it's real estate investing, seek out someone who has already successfully done it, not someone who just aspires to do it. Then, listen carefully to what they say.

As we've covered, nothing worth succeeding at comes for free and enduring patience will be the price you're paying in this particular process. The extra time you spend doing your due diligence will help ensure you're meeting your goal in a meaningful and sustainable way. And, in the end it will actually wind up saving you much time from going down the wrong road. You absolutely must work hard at this process and use the power of your mind to stop you along the way. There is no way around it.

As you're beginning to practice weighing fact from opinion, you may also begin practicing how you speak about topics as well. Many times, those who excel at the ability to determine fact versus opinion are also skilled at not posing their opinions as facts. If they're speaking their opinion on something, they will be quite transparent that it is just that—an opinion.

Additionally, when someone is asking your opinion on a subject, if you are not well-versed on it, instead of coming up with something on a whim, or stating what you perceive as the popular opinion, simply state that you don't know as you are not an expert on that subject. Giving an honest answer will bring you a lot of respect from others.

It's key to mention here that the way you've become trained to absorb information is partly determined by physical heredity and partly by social heredity, the first of which you're born with (think, left-brained versus right-brained) and the latter of which you're exposed to throughout your lifetime due to your social surroundings.

Without realizing it, there is a chance that you've blindly accepted others' opinions as your own throughout your lifetime based on a combination of both your physical and social heredity. You can take back the control, though. Use your mind to do so.

You should always exercise your own free will in making decisions or taking sides on something. Rather than saying "Well, my family/friends feel this way, so I do as well," really consider what that means to you. Just as your thoughts hold great power in keeping your mind positive or negative, your thoughts also hold great power in determining whether there is validity to the things you're hearing and seeing and what direction you should move in to effectively meet your goal.

Be mindful of how your past experiences and social interactions may have already swayed your thoughts on a decision that's critical to your goal. If you've determined an example, focus in on it and try to come to a new decision without any of those social determinants. You might find that by focusing in on it in a new light, your free will points you in a completely different direction than you were heading, with your own thoughts leading you down the road to success.

CHAPTER 13

Finding and Maintaining Your Focus

If you're unable to remain focused on your goal, how will you ever achieve it? Just as with the other topics we've discussed so far, the ability to get focused, and then to remain focused, is essential to achieving success. It's important that we all know and understand how to accomplish this as well as the rationale behind why focus is so critical.

Let's start with an example. Not too long ago, a friend came to us for business advice. He was frustrated, as he'd been attempting to launch three unique small businesses and wasn't finding success at any of them, despite putting a great deal of time and energy into all three. He was tired and ready to give up. Our advice to him: Pick one of the three and focus all of your attention there. It was very ambitious of him to want to launch all three businesses at the same time, but it would be nearly impossible for him to find success with any of them if his focus was divided. What he needed to do was hone his attention in on one business, develop a concrete plan to grow it and then begin moving the needle.

You can probably guess what happened next. He took that advice, ran with it and now that first business is booming. With that business up and running, he has moved himself into more of a general oversight position and he's moving on to focus on the second business. Our best guess is that second business will be just as successful and then he'll be able to focus on the third. You see, it is never too big of a dream to say you want to start multiple businesses or accomplish multiple goals—continue to use your imagination and dream as large as you would like! The main takeaway from this example is that success can be best attained if you're able to fully focus on one big goal at a time.

How can you remain fully focused on your goal when there are so many things in your life that are conflicting for your attention? We get it. Life is busy. Maybe you're currently in a position where you're attempting to juggle a career with family while maintaining a social life and furthering your education. Or, maybe you're trying to balance playing sports while you're in school and trying to focus on being accepted to your desired college. It all may seem too much—especially if your goal is separate from all these things. But it can be done, with the right focus and attention.

A man by the name of Ryan Blair once said, "If it's important you'll find a way. If not, you will find an excuse."[65] This heavily applies to our conversation here on focus. If your goal is truly something you have an obsession to succeed at, you will find time to focus on it. If you're finding over and over again that your goal and your plan to achieve it are falling to the back burner, you may consider whether this goal is one you really want—in your heart of hearts. If you aren't finding time to focus on it, it's possible it's not something you really want. If you're obsessed with achieving your goal, your focus will naturally follow.

"Successful people maintain a positive focus in life no matter what is going on around them. They stay focused on their past successes rather than their past failures, and on the next action steps they need to take to get them closer to the fulfillment of their goals rather than all the other distractions that life presents to them."
—*Jack Canfield*[66]

Once you've found what it is you really want to achieve and you're committed to getting focused on it, the power of your mind begins to come back into play. Just as you've become accustomed to blocking negative thoughts from your mind (which would attract negative things), your ability to stay focused on positive thoughts and outcomes will bring about positive things and outcomes.

Despite the many obligations you have beyond the achievement of your goal, you must have your mind heavily focused on achieving your goal if you want to find success. You must free up mental space for it. There can be no other way. Your focus should be on your goal at most moments throughout a given day. Let it be something you wake up thinking about. Let it be something to go to sleep thinking about. And fill in thoughts of achieving your goal in moments in between.

In the last chapter, we talked about why it is so important to separate important information we're receiving every day from the unimportant information we've receiving. We're doing this for the purpose of staying focused. The better you get at weeding through that information, the more time you'll free up to focus on achieving your goal. This works in reverse too. Ideally, you're going to get to a point where you're so busy with thoughts of your goal that you won't even have the time to focus on any unimportant information that comes your way.

"The key to success is to focus our conscious mind on things we desire not things we fear."
—Brian Tracy[67]

Aside from the great deal of unimportant information that comes our way in a given day that could distract our focus if we allow it, there is something else that also ends up distracting many people as well: Worrying. Worry ends up taking up a lot of a person's time, if they allow it to. Many times, the things we're wasting time worrying about are not even real. People tend to fabricate scenarios in their mind about "worst-case situations" and—instead of creating that essential positive space in their mind—they're clogging it up with negativity. When you're fighting against a negative idea you've come up with in your mind, you're essentially giving it power. You're focusing on it enough so that it's taken up space in your mind. You can deny yourself of what you want and distract your focus by making up a problem or enemy that isn't actually there. So, don't allow that to happen. When worry creeps in, send it away immediately, and replace it with thoughts of a successful outcome.

"Worry never robs tomorrow of its sorrow, it only saps today of its joy."
—Leo F. Buscaglia[68]

Whatever it is that you're focusing on—in this case your goal—soon becomes the dominant force in your mind, outweighing all others. With the right focus, when things happen in your given day your brain becomes trained to immediately think "How does this pertain to my goal?"

When you're fully focused, you're able to sharpen your ability to quickly make decisions. You're also able to quickly and more simply assess a situation to understand if your current plan is not working out and why, and how to aim to be more successful in your revised plan. The ability to remain focused ensures that you're solution-oriented. Anyone who is fully focused on a goal can be posed with any challenge and immediately begin to come up with ways around it. Their mind, at this point, knows no other way.

> *"Don't dwell on what went wrong. Instead, focus on what to do next. Spend your energies on moving forward toward finding the answer."*
> —*Denis Waitley*[69]

Many people go through life without focus of any meaningful kind. These are the people you know who believe things just happen to them, and they go with the flow. They don't believe they have control, so they don't attempt to take it. As we know though, each of us has control. All we have to do is take it, and point it in the right direction, in a focused manner. Think of it as a magnifying glass that focuses the rays and energy of the sun on a specific spot so well that it can actually start a fire. When you make it a point to focus your thoughts and actions on success—no matter what success means to you—you will attract the energy, things and circumstances to start the fire under your goals.

There are some easy ways you can get and remain focused:

Audit Your Time

Busy lives can result in limited time for focus on your goal… if you allow it. We guarantee you'll be able to free up time if you take a close look at the things you're currently spending time on. In our earlier chapter on self-discipline, we recommended an exercise where you should write down everything you do while you are awake for the course of three full days and outline how long you are doing each activity for. This will give a good sample of what you typically spend your time on, and without a doubt, there will be activities in there that you can pinpoint as wasted time. Identify them and use that time more wisely—to focus on your goal. Ultimately, the mission here is that there will be no wasted time, because you quite literally won't have time for it.

Turn Off Your Cell Phone

While using the time auditing exercise, likely you'll find that some, or perhaps even all, of your deemed wasted time is spent on your cell phone. This could include the use of games, social media, texting friends and the like. It's something that's worth its own individual mention here as time on a cell phone can pull focus away from your goal in mass quantities. What's more, it can also be a distraction—you can be fully focused on a task for your goal, but if your cell phone keeps ringing or buzzing with messages, it's going to distract you each and every time. To stay as focused as possible, try turning off your cell phone at designated times to work on your goal. You'll find the time spent focusing on the task at hand will be so much more productive just from doing so.

Set Deadlines (If You Haven't Yet Already)

We've already covered in previous chapters how setting (and meeting) deadlines can be beneficial to you. If you haven't already done so, you should absolutely be setting deadlines for yourself as part of your plan. Setting deadlines is an effective way of keeping one's self focused. If you know you have something due by a certain time, your focus will immediately heighten and remain steadfast until you've completed it. Deadlines prevent focus from being stolen from your goal and redirected elsewhere. Once you've set those deadlines, that focus will force you to put everything you have into meeting them. Being accountable to someone else for meeting your deadlines is also an effective way to make sure that you focus and follow through.

Avoid Multitasking

Many people claim to be excellent at multitasking; however, studies have shown that only two percent of people are effective multitaskers. It's because of a lack of full focus. For the best results in staying focused and successfully completing a task, avoid multitasking and instead put that focus on one thing at a time. You'll find yourself completing tasks more quickly and effectively.

Lean on (Positive!) People Around You

If you find your focus is lacking despite all attempts to reinvigorate it, try leaning on those around you. Sit and chat with them and talk about the current progress toward your goal and next steps. A simple conversation can be enough to get your focus sharpened again.

> *"One day the Zen master wanted to show his students a new technique of shooting an arrow. He told his students to cover his eyes with a cloth and then he shot his arrow. When he opened his eyes, he saw the target with no arrow in it and when he looked at his students, they looked embarrassed because their teacher had missed.*
>
> *The Zen master asked them, 'What lesson do you think I intend to teach you all today?' They answered, 'We thought you would show us how to shoot at the target without looking.'*
>
> *The Zen master said, 'No, I taught you that if you want to be successful in life, don't forget the target. You have to keep an eye on the target, otherwise you may miss a good opportunity in life.' They looked at each other, impressed with the lesson."*
>
> *—Unknown*

As a reminder, keep your mind busy with thoughts that will help you to reach your goal, and not those that will distract you. Like attracts like, so use your focus in a positive way and you will receive positive results. And the best part is that if you put your focus and attention on what it is you want, you will by nature be deflecting the things you don't want at the same time.

CHAPTER 14

Using Hurdles to Your Advantage

In the year 2000, Netflix—a company that was only three years old at the time—was a service built on mailing DVD rentals to its subscribers. With a giant company like Blockbuster nearly monopolizing the world of DVD rentals, and before the time where online streaming had taken off, Netflix was losing money quickly.[70] *Its co-founders, Marc Randolph and Reed Hastings, were adamant on finding success and came up with a solid plan to make money, rather than continue to lose it. They would persistently request a meeting with Blockbuster CEO John Antioco until they were able to get in front of him—and they would offer him a deal: Buy out Netflix for $50 million and use its established online presence and know-how to build out Blockbuster.com. At that time, Netflix had already predicted the rise of the internet in movie rentals while Blockbuster had not been as prepared. To Netflix's CEOs, this seemed like an excellent deal for Blockbuster.*

Antioco did not see it that way. He rejected their offer. At the time, Randolph and Hastings had considered this potential buy-out their only way out of a sinking ship, however when *faced with this hurdle, they realized they could either consider this a failure and give up, or figure out another way to make Netflix a success. Naturally, they chose the latter. Instead of allowing this hurdle to drown them, they realized this gave them further fuel for their fire to succeed. Because of their unwillingness to give up, and rather their desire to revise their plan of action and continue moving forward, Netflix ultimately prevailed over Blockbuster. Today Netflix is worth an estimated $130 billion.*[70]

Along the path to success of any kind, a person is bound to face hurdles and defeats. This is an inevitable part of the process to achieving success. Another clear difference between someone who finds success and someone who does not is how they view hurdles and defeats. For the successful person, a hurdle is seen as just that—a road bump that can, with varying degrees of effort, be overcome. In fact, for the successful person, their mind not only knows they can get past it, they are able to analyze the situation and also find a *benefit* in the hurdle. For the unsuccessful person, hurdles are viewed as failures. The hurdles prevent the unsuccessful person from continuing to believe they can accomplish something. Instead, they solely view the hurdle as a negative thing and it ends in them giving up on what they've been trying to achieve.

Once again, we're right back to the power of the mind. How we view and think about a particular situation dictates how we feel about it and what we, in turn, do about it. Throughout this book, we're assuring you success in anything you want to accomplish, and this is primarily through the practice of training your mind to accept no other way. When you're sure, with full certainty, that you're going to accomplish a goal, you must also be sure that any hurdle that comes in your way of accomplishing that goal can be overcome—and can provide a benefit to you. Because it can.

We should start by acknowledging the fact that hurdles and failure are two very different things. A hurdle, as we'll come to think of it from this point forward, can be worked around and can provide a benefit. It is only a temporary setback. A failure is only something known to those who are unable to achieve success—they view those setbacks as permanent defeat. Failure should not even be in your vocabulary at this point, because on your path to success, it simply doesn't exist. Failure is not an option… only if we allow it to be in our minds. And we're not going to.

Here's an example. Let's consider for a moment a person whose goal is to become the Vice President of their department at work. This person has taken all the necessary steps we've discussed throughout this book so far in order to achieve that goal and they're continuing to work hard to achieve it, no matter what it takes. Now let's say that coveted Vice President position vacates. This person is sure that the stellar work and long hours they've been putting in, combined with their positive mental attitude, will mean they're a shoo-in to move into that role. However, let's say the company selects a colleague of theirs to fill the Vice President position instead. They can now choose one of two roads. On path one, they can view this as a hurdle and a situation they can find a benefit in. On the other path, they can let self-pity overcome them, consider this a failure and forget about their goal all together. What path would the success-minded person take?

> *"What looks like a loss may be the very event which is subsequently responsible for helping to produce the major achievement in your life."*
> *—Srully Blotnick*[71]

In this situation, a success-minded person, upon finding out the news that they had been passed over for the position, would follow the first path. While anyone would likely have a feeling of disappointment when first finding out the news, it's what happens next that clearly separates those who end up successful and those who will not. If the person in this example chose path one, they'd immediately begin to examine the situation and revise their plan to achieve their goal. For example, maybe upon closer look, they would find out that the colleague who was chosen was better connected to someone in a senior level position at the company. An unsuccessful person could view this as an unfair advantage, but the successful person could use this as an opportunity to encourage themselves to attend more frequent networking events and focus in on relationship-building. Down the road, this may lead them to another, even better, job position. It's all about mindset and how a positive mindset can trigger positive action and positive results.

The more a person prepares themselves for how to mentally handle hurdles while things are going well in their path to success, the better equipped they will be when they are unexpectedly faced with one. A tried and true practice is to mentally establish this positive way of thinking about hurdles prior to any appearing. In the moment, without having trained our brains to think about hurdles in a benefit-oriented manner, a person might view the hurdle in a negative light.

> *Our relative Joey, a rising star in the real estate development world, was put in charge of a large development project by a real estate investment company at just 26 years old. Just as the project was nearly complete, an outside association that governed the greater area decided they didn't like some of the project's commercial tenants. This came as quite a surprise to Joey, as these details had been worked out before his project even started.*
>
> *What came next was a big hurdle to say the least. The association was made up of 330 high rise condominium owners, all of whom were going up against Joey alone.*

After a yearlong battle, that took up almost all his time, Joey prevailed and won the fight. He then successfully sold off the project as planned and the investment company made a very handsome profit. The hurdle was overcome and rewards were received—all because of his persistent efforts. Joey's ability to overcome the hurdle and not give up did not go unnoticed by the investment group. He was promoted to Vice President and very shortly thereafter became a partner in the company. Today, he is extremely successful.

If you wait until you have a hurdle on your front doorstep to mentally prepare yourself, it's possible you might get caught up in the adversity and allow it to bring you down. This is simply because our minds are innately hardwired this way. When things don't go a person's way, their brain is pre-set, in a sense, to get upset and feel bad about it. However, if this person already has the mental know-how to manage hurdles positively, they'll be prepared to work around—and see the benefit in—any hurdle that comes their way.

When a hurdle is placed in your way, the first question you should ask yourself is, "Where is the benefit in this for me?" If the answer is not immediately apparent, ask yourself, "What can I do to turn this into a benefit?"

If you ask yourself those questions, and keep repeating them over and over, you will always find a benefit—an opportunity that will bring you even closer to your goal than if you had not experienced the hurdle or temporary setback in the first place. Remember the Netflix's story? That's exactly what it exemplifies.

"Our strength grows out of our weakness. Not until we are pricked and stung and sorely shot at, awakens the indignation which arms itself with secret forces. A great man is always willing to be little. Whilst he sits on the cushion of advantages

*he goes to sleep. When he is pushed, tormented, defeated,
he has a chance to learn something; he has been put on his
wits; on his manhood; he has gained facts; learned from
his ignorance; been cured of the insanity of conceit; has got
moderation and real skill."*
—*Ralph Waldo Emerson*[72]

Benefits can be found in each and every hurdle faced on your path to success. If you look hard enough, they will always be there. Sometimes the benefit will be very small and sometimes it will be very large, but either way, there will be a benefit of some kind. Every time we are faced with a hurdle, in addition to the benefit we will receive from it, we also grow as a person. Our strength is built by our ability to overcome adversities.

As you learn to overcome these hurdles, it becomes a habit for you. No matter what happens, you will always expect to somehow have a winning outcome, in every situation.

*Another excellent real-world example is that of Angela Logan.
About a decade ago, Angela—a Teaneck, NJ woman—was
about to lose her home.*[73] *With three children to take care of
and potentially no place for them and her husband to live in
the near future, Angela decided to bake her way out of the
bad situation. She turned her home's kitchen into a bakery,
cooking various cake recipes and selling the goods. People
in her community and beyond immediately responded and
there was an influx of people not only willing to help spread
her story, but also those willing to purchase her baked goods.
As for her family, they were right there helping her hands-on
to take orders, chop apples, deliver orders and more.*

*Simultaneously, she was bringing in money on the side
braiding hair in a salon. She worked hard doing both as*

*simply a means of preventing foreclosure on her house.
And, that she did. Not only was she able to save her house—
after years of selling her cakes online and at local farmers'
markets—she opened her very own bakery which is now
continuing to thrive in her community.*[73]

Sometimes a benefit of encountering a hurdle along your path to success is the need for self-evaluation. Perhaps you've been taking your eye off of the prize a bit and the hurdle is stopping you in your tracks and reminding you of it. For instance, perhaps you have been allowing a negative mindset to creep in without realizing it. Perhaps you've allowed your verbal and non-verbal skills to slip. Maybe your enthusiasm has been severely lacking. If you encounter a hurdle, consider if you've been neglecting any of the success lessons we've been discussing in the book by evaluating yourself completely. Reference earlier chapters of this book as needed. Remember, all the success lessons discussed in the book are critical to success, so allow that time to evaluate if you're paying adequate attention to and acting on all of them to the best of your ability.

If you encounter a hurdle, here are some quick things you can remind yourself of in relevance to our success lessons in order to overcome it:

- If a limiting belief is holding you back, acknowledge what it is and then begin to erase it and replace it with a new, positive belief.
- If your positive mindset has started to skew negative, re-center it. Our minds should always be focused on the things we do want in life, not the things we do not want. Remember, how you feel about the thought you are thinking tells you if that thought is taking you toward or away from what you desire.
- If you've lost sight of your goal, focus in on it yet again. Use this time to make sure your goal is truly something you have a

real desire to achieve. A hurdle should be further igniting that burning desire. Once you confirm to yourself that you want it, your eyes should always be on that prize and you should be thinking as often as you can about achieving that goal.

- If you've lost your motivation to achieve your goal, remember that you cannot receive anything of worth in life without putting work into it. Everything costs something—and in this case it will be your hard work. Achieving your goal is going to require your blood, sweat and tears, and you must be consistently motivated in order to give it your all, both in your mind and actions.

- It's incredibly important to make decisions using both emotion and reasoning, and to make those decisions quickly. If you've been approaching your decision-making, relevant to your goal, in a different manner than that, it's time to make a change. Feel the joy of achieving your goal and make the best decisions that you can toward its attainment.

- If you haven't had time to work on your goal recently, make time. A goal without any time spent working toward it will remain unreached.

- For a successful person, a hurdle is not a failure. *We cannot stress this enough.*

Another clear benefit of encountering a hurdle could be a realization that it's time to revise your plan. It's possible your plan was flawed in ways you may have not previously noticed as things were going well. When you encounter a hurdle, instead of focusing on what the hurdle was and how it's setting you back, you should always be thinking of what you can now do to get around it—and many times you will find this, subsequently, will require a necessary revision to your plan.

"Failure is simply the opportunity to begin again, this time more intelligently."
—Henry Ford[74]

We've continued to say this but here we go again—hurdles and failures are not the same thing. While a failure may encourage an unsuccessful person to give up on their dreams, success-minded people will see the same event as a hurdle that they can benefit from. *Under no circumstances should you let a hurdle allow you to give up on a goal.*

Let's look at another example. A person had a goal to start their own local business. After a few months, it became apparent to this person that the business was losing, not making money. If they viewed this as a failure, they might close the business doors and resort back to their old job that they weren't happy in, just to make sure they were collecting a consistent paycheck. If they instead viewed this as a hurdle, they would re-evaluate their business plan, and keep moving forward with persistence and a more strategic approach until their dream was accomplished. Remember, "Whatever the mind can conceive and believe, it can achieve."

"Winners never quit, and quitters never win."
—Vince Lombardi[75]

While we've now fully delved into how we should handle hurdles as they come our way, it's vital that we remember a lesson we've previously discussed about not allowing worry to creep into our minds. If we're constantly worried about what the next hurdle we'll encounter might be, what we are in turn doing is attracting that which we fear. There is a difference between being prepared to have the right mindset should a hurdle present itself and *worrying* that a hurdle will present itself. It's critical that we know and understand that difference and use it to our advantage.

In the end, there should be no reason a hurdle of any kind or size should allow any of us to give up on what we want out of life. You've made it this far into the book—we know that you want big success, no matter what success means to you individually. So go after it. Nothing can stand in your way with the power of your mind on your side. And we mean nothing.

Here's another example. In 2012, the U.S. Department of Justice forced the State of Virginia to begin shutting down its large institutions throughout the state that housed over 1,000 of its mentally challenged or special needs persons. The Justice Department considered these types of facilities, each housing hundreds of individuals with special needs, to be detrimental to the individuals. They demanded that the State of Virginia implement and execute a plan to not only close all of those institutions, but also to relocate the individuals to communities where they could live a more fulfilling life, outside the confines of these large institutions.

While this was a great humanitarian move, it was not particularly great for the employees who had worked at those institutions who were about to lose their jobs. One of those employees, Mark, was married with two children and had a substantial mortgage, and was about to have no income.

Mark was a friend of Bob, one of our close relatives, and shortly after receiving the news that his workplace would be closing, Mark reached out to Bob and explained his situation and an idea he had. Although there were a lot of well-established companies that were currently handling housing and caring for these individuals with special needs who were getting relocated, Mark felt he could obtain the proper licensing to operate a home for these individuals. Having deep knowledge of the specific needs of these individuals, his idea incorporated offering them the right type of home (e.g., ranch-style, no stairs, proper ramps, etc.) and could successfully run it as a profit. Mark wanted a better product than his competitors to better attract the clientele. He also had a goal of providing a standard of living that would far surpass what these individuals were accustomed to or what was currently available.

What Mark lacked was the capital to get this idea off the ground. He asked Bob if he was interested in participating in the project, or had the ability to fund the project, land, construction, furnishing, licensing and so on for the home. Low and behold, Bob was able to partner with Mark and fund the project, and years later, they now have nine homes and several related ancillary businesses.

Because of Mark's ability to turn a hurdle into a benefit, he has built and owns an extremely successful business with substantial earnings. Not only is he living his happiest life, he has enhanced the quality of life for those living in his facilities and peace of mind for their families and loved ones.

There is always a way to benefit from every hurdle so remember to look closely for it. If you can't find it, keep looking. Remaining benefit-focused is key. Continue to remind yourself that any time a hurdle arises that something good will come out of it, without a doubt.

A great example of overcoming a physical hurdle is that of Franklin D. Roosevelt. As an adult, Roosevelt developed polio and became paralyzed from the waist down. He could have very easily allowed this to affect his mental health and prevent him for achieving what he wanted out of life—but he did just the opposite. Not only did he not let his paralysis kill his spirit, he went on to become the 32nd President of the United States and was beloved by many. His positive attitude and can-do personality helped navigate the country through the Great Depression and much of World War II. What's more, Roosevelt also helped create the country's National Foundation for Infantile Paralysis which funded rehab programs for others who'd experienced the same disease and effects he had, as well as vaccinations. Not only did he overcome what could have been perceived as a hurdle in his life, he then used what he'd gone through to help benefit others.[76]

CHAPTER 15

The Power of a Creative Mind

It's likely you know a person in your life who always seems to come up with the best, out-of-the-box ideas. It's almost as if their brain works on a different frequency than others around him or her. What's more, this person not only thinks of great ideas, he or she takes action on them as well. Depending on how they're using their creativity, it's possible this person has been finding great success in their life, too.

How can creativity lead to success? Let your mind travel momentarily to some of the most successful business people in the world today. Consider what it is that made them their fortune. What you'll find is that many of them got where they are, in part, because they came up with an idea (or a unique twist on an existing idea) that skyrocketed them into fortune.

"Creative thinking is today's most prized, profit-producing possession of any individual, corporation or country. It has the capacity to change you, your business or country and the world."
—Robert P. Crawford[77]

Naturally, the other success tactics we've discussed so far, in addition to what we'll discuss in future chapters, must all work together with creativity. But creativity is such a key piece to the puzzle, particularly when it comes to professional goals. And unfortunately many people do not realize the power creativity can hold.

If your goal involves starting or growing a business, you know just how necessary creativity is. If you did things the same exact way as your existing competitors, how could you ever find meaningful success? You simply must do something different to stand out from the crowd, and in turn, build the business as large as possible.

You might be reading this right now and saying to yourself, "Well, I'm not a creative person, so this isn't going to work for me."

Let us tell you here that we *all* have the ability to tap into the power of creativity. Each of us has an imagination that can dream up incredibly distinct plans and outcomes. Many times, it just requires giving ourselves dedicated time to tap into it.

We've said it time and time again—there is great power in thought. Many people struggle to tap into their creativity because they don't allow themselves time to think. Hopefully you've already been excelling at training your mind to be positive by dedicating time for positive thoughts and gratitude as we've discussed, but dedicated thought to the creative process should be considered a separate tool for success. And it doesn't have to take up a lot of your time. But it will be worthwhile for you.

> *"Clean out a corner in your mind and creativity will instantly fill in."*
> *—Dee Hock*[78]

In the morning, we're already in the practice of setting our mind in a positive direction and noting what it is we are grateful for, in addition to what things we *will* be grateful for. If you feel as though your creativity could use a boost, it's a good practice to now dedicate a few minutes at some other point throughout your day to brainstorm. It can be just a few minutes, if that's all you have. Come into your personal brainstorming session with a topic that needs your creative juices, and if you fully dedicate yourself to that topic during that time, you will—with certainty—begin to find your imagination growing and growing. Ask yourself the right questions, such as, "What is the answer to...?" or, "How do I...?" You will be amazed with the results.

It's also a good practice to avoid activities that drain your creativity and leave your mind in an otherwise idle statement. This includes limiting excessive television and smartphone use, for example.

Now let's speak to those reading this who are already churning out plenty of ideas using their power of creativity, but feel as though none of those ideas can be put into action for one reason or another.

Do any of the below statements seem familiar to you?

- *This idea has never been done before, so it won't work.*
- *There are too many competitors in this space, so it won't work.*
- *This idea is going to cost too much money, so it won't work.*
- *I don't have the skillset to execute this idea, so it won't work.*
- *This idea will require too many people and resources to get off the ground, so it won't work.*

We'll say this flat out to you right here and now: *Stop coming up with excuses!* That's just what these statements are. Those people whose minds stop them in their tracks from bringing their ideas to fruition are those who believe their imagination is thinking too big. Well, it's not. Our imaginations are endless. Through the success habits outlined in this book, your imagination can never think too big. Anything is possible. If you continue to believe your creativity is pushing you too far and too big, you'll never be able to achieve anything big.

> *"If you can dream it, you can do it."*
> *—Walt Disney*[79]

Those statements we mentioned are statements of self-doubt. If you're using those phrases or other similar ones that make you feel as though your goal and ideas to achieve it are impossible, it means your inner faith in yourself is lacking. This eats away at your positive mindset, and the cycle continues. We need the cycle to be heading the other way—in a positive way that fuels inner faith and makes any idea you're able to come up with achievable. Remember, if you can conceive it, you can achieve it. But you must first believe it.

Sometimes, maybe the questioning of your ideas is fueled by those around you. It's possible that you're often encountering people who drain you of creativity and make you question otherwise sound ideas. Remember those "dream stealers" we talked about in the book's introduction? This is them, too. Managing people who squash your creativity, or in essence steal your dreams, is just as important as managing those who are negative in other ways. Often these dream stealers can be easily spotted as those who shoot down your ideas and tend to be a negative force in your mental space. As noted earlier, a practice here is to spend minimal time talking to these dream stealers where possible, and otherwise to put up those walls in your mind and not let their words and actions seep into your mental space.

Consider the story of how FedEx began. Fred Smith came up with an interesting idea back in the 1960s while attending Yale University, but it wasn't particularly well-received.[80] *In an economics term paper, he wrote about the concept of overnight delivery—a business idea for which he thought there was a growing need. When he handed the paper in, he didn't quite get the response he'd hoped for. His professor famously said in response to the paper: "The concept is interesting and well-formed, but in order to earn better than a 'C', the idea must be feasible."*

Years later, Fred decided to pursue that very idea despite the negative feedback he'd originally received. And, thankfully he did! Thanks to Fred, FedEx was established, changing the speed at which people could receive deliveries. FedEx was the world's first overnight delivery service and today continues to make billions of dollars a year.

All of this is not to say that as you're kicking off your path to your goal and coming up with ideas you shouldn't be honest with yourself about whether the ideas make sense. Not all ideas you come up with will be good ones, but what we're telling you here is that any idea—no matter how big or small—is worth a thorough examination. If the only potential issue you're coming up with regarding an idea is that there may be hurdles in executing it—or that others around you cannot see the potential—these are certainly not reasons to dismiss it!

We're already equipped with the proper mindset to overcome hurdles, so don't let that stand in your way. The beauty of creativity, too, is that it can be used to *overcome* hurdles. The more you practice getting your mind into a creative state, the easier you'll be able to tap into it when faced with a hurdle of any kind. Your creativity will help guide you around the hurdle by coming up with unique ideas to do so. Creativity can put you back on the right course to finding success. That's the greatest thing about creativity. It can truly help you overcome anything in your way. If you're driven to succeed, you're going to succeed—every time.

Those who are best able to channel their creativity to achieve success are those who have a passion to do the otherwise impossible. If everyone's minds constantly told them, "Well, that's never been done before, so it's probably not going to work," then nothing of value in invention, for instance, would have ever been accomplished. There would be no electricity, no internet, no automobiles, and many other necessities we have in society today if it wasn't for people who were able to channel their creativity, think outside of the box and let nothing stand in their way of achieving their goal.

According to Dr. Napoleon Hill's "Think and Grow Rich," when Guglielmo Marconi announced he had figured out a way to transmit electronic messages from one place to another without the aid of wires, his friends had him committed to a mental institution.[81] *He eventually convinced a doctor there that he, in fact, was able to do just so and challenged the doctor to let him out of the institution and to accompany him to his laboratory so he could demonstrate it. The doctor, along with several others, were among the first to witness communication through the ether, without the aid of wires. This was the birth of radio communications that would eventually connect the world, and subsequently lead to the development of television, Wi-Fi and cell phones, just to name a few.*

Not only did Marconi display a true sense of creativity in his invention, but he also showed an ability to overcome any dream stealers who were standing in his way. This marks a truly successful person.

The more focused you remain on your goal, the more you will have a will to make it work, no matter what. The more time you spend thinking about achieving your goal and how you'll get there, the more time your brain is spending thinking of unique ways to do so. As we've said many times, your plan to achieve your goal can be altered along the way as needed, and sometimes it's altered because you've used your creativity to spark a new idea that's going to work *even better* than the one you originally intended.

What if the ideas you're coming up with are similar to ideas that already exist? That's not a problem at all. In fact, that's how most ideas are born—by considering pieces of information a person already knows and combining them to come up with something even bigger and better. A lot of times, the best use of creativity in a business setting is an idea that builds on something that already exists, and either makes it better, or perhaps more convenient for the user. Think of cell phone technology right now as an example. It continues to build on what's already in existence and continues to become more convenient for users and more profitable for those coming up with the ideas.

> *"Imagination is more important than knowledge."*
> *—Albert Einstein*[82]

Try using your creativity to succeed in your goal by leaning on information you already know to be true. This can lead to you finding a brand-new way of approaching things that has never been considered before. And, it can prove to be a whole lot more profitable than what's already in existence. Remember, through the use of a creative mind, our imaginations can come up with the biggest, most wild things, if we allow it.

Even the most creative minds will need inspiration from time to time. Inspiration for creativity can come as easily as watching people around you. If you look closely, there are so many sources of inspiration in the people you know personally. Maybe it's your co-worker who tends to share ideas in meetings. Listen when he or she speaks. Maybe it's your friend who always seems to be able to come up with solutions to difficult problems. Talk to them often and pay attention to how they come up with these solutions.

Other times, inspiration can come for hearing or reading stories about people you don't know personally. Let's look at this story of how a creative mind—coupled with motivation and enthusiasm—was able to spark what is now one of the world's most innovative and successful companies:

In 1994, at just 30 years old, Jeff Bezos' creative mind saw the potential of the Internet as an up and coming way to shop for merchandise. As he saw it, the appeal of consumers being able to shop without having to leave their home posed great potential. He began brainstorming and then hit the ground running. He quit his full-time job on Wall Street and convinced his parents to invest a large percentage of their life savings so that he could fund his company, Amazon.

Bezos began Amazon humbly by shipping books from his garage to those who purchased them through his online site. By 1997 he took the company public and by 1999 he was named Time Magazine's Person of the Year, for popularizing online shopping. Now, Amazon has become the online capital for buying merchandise of all kinds. His creative mind, backed by inner faith, enthusiasm and motivation has today made Bezos the richest person in the world. Not only that, it's made the lives of millions and millions of people who use Amazon much more convenient.[83]

It's worth mentioning here as well that often people will give up on their big ideas, not because they feel any self-doubt necessarily or doubt from others, but because they're—let's just say it… lazy.

We all must understand that nothing comes for free. It's going to take a lot of hard work to achieve anything of significance in life. It's going to be a lot easier to quit than it will to press forward. Those who remain motivated and focused will prevail over those who lose steam. An idea without any continued action taken on it will forever remain just an idea.

> *"It's better to have tried and failed than to have never tried at all."*
> *—Unknown*

I'm sure by this point you're beginning to see how all of our chapters and success habits are connected to one another. Each habit builds on the next. By continuing to combine them, you'll find nothing but success.

CHAPTER 16

A Healthy Mind and Body

A woman we worked with some time ago seemed to discuss potential health ailments more than anyone we'd ever previously met. In fact, in our very first conversation with her she let us know about a heart attack she'd had a few years prior and how she always lived in fear that she would have another. During our next conversation, she was feeling under the weather and was scared she was coming down with strep throat. In our next chat, she was having strange symptoms that she was sure were the result of shingles. This went on and on quite regularly.

In some cases, she would come down with the illness she so feared. However, even in the times when her health fear would not be realized, she consistently proved to be in a negative state of mind. She believed negative things would happen to her, so she was attracting negativity into her life. Living this way was setting her back not only in the workplace, but it was also diminishing her sense of overall happiness outside of work as well, as we gathered in further conversations with her. While we never asked her how she, in particular, measured success, we can be certain that no matter how she measured it—she was not achieving it.

It may come as little surprise to you based on what you now know about the power of the mind that there is a strong connection between your mind and your body. It is believed that having an on-going negative attitude toward physical health can, in some cases, result in negative health outcomes. And, as noted in the previous example, even in cases when negative health outcomes don't arise from this kind of thinking, at minimum the person is setting their mental well-being on a negative track. As we've come to understand, a negative mind will make the attainment of success in any capacity impossible.

> *"There are many aspects to success; material wealth is only one component…. But success also includes good health, energy and enthusiasm for life, fulfilling relationships, creative freedom, emotional and psychological stability, a sense of well-being, and peace of mind."*
> *—Deepak Chopra*[84]

The more positive your mind is, the better off your body will be as a whole. The more negative your mind is, the worse off your body will be. Your thoughts affect *everything* in your life—physical well-being included.

If you needed yet another reason to keep yourself in a positive mindset, there it is. Every time you put in work to ensure your mind is remaining positive, you're doing right by your overall health and well-being as well. And, the healthier you are overall, the more energized you'll be toward achieving your goal. It's a win-win situation.

Likewise, if you're living a healthy lifestyle—inclusive of a healthy diet and regular exercise—you're going to experience positive benefits. According to the Anxiety and Depression Association of America,[85] in addition to exercise helping to relieve stress and anxiety and having the potential to boost self-esteem and improve sleeping habits, it also releases those feel-good endorphins in your brain that we've all heard of, making you feel happy. This overall better state of being and level of happiness can be channeled into the achievement of your goal.

Additionally, a study out of Leeds Metropolitan University[86] in the United Kingdom showed a direct connection between exercise and success in the workplace. The study showed that those who used the gym at their workplace during the day were more productive and had better interactions with their coworkers. Those who exercised also were happier after work as well.

No matter how you approach it, getting your mind and body into a healthy place takes work. We've talked in previous chapters about tactics you can use to both establish and maintain a positive mindset. When it comes to keeping your body healthy, it may be beneficial to speak to a verified expert in the field, perhaps reaching out to your primary care physician, a nutritionist and/or personal trainer or other health care professional to outline the best plan for you. Make sure those you're seeking counsel from are, in fact, experts before acting on their advice and guidance.

Unfortunately, we cannot tell you confidently that keeping a positive mindset day in and day out will prevent disease or illness, as there are factors about each of our bodies that we have little to no control over. Likely, there is someone you've known, for example, who is an incredibly positive person and was diagnosed with an unfavorable illness. Sometimes, our bodies act in ways completely outside of our control. What we can confidently remind you of is the one thing in our bodies that we have *complete and total control over…* our mind. That is an important thing to remind ourselves of over, and over and over. And we must take action on grooming our mind again, and again and again. Those who are able to maintain a positive mindset— even despite a health ailment of any kind—are the real winners in life.

The more positive our mindset is and the healthier lifestyle we're living in general, the less we'll be worrying about the "what ifs" in life, and the more we'll be focusing on our goals and achieving them. The more we're focused on the positive, the less time we'll have for the negative, like worrying and complaining. Many people go through their given day looking for things to worry or complain about. This wears away at their mental health, and often, can even affect their physical health as well. Worries and complaints will be (and should always be!) left at the door when you're living positively and healthy, through both mind and body. There is no time for worry, complaints or even excuses.

> *"The secret to health for both, body and mind, is not to mourn*
> *the past, not to worry about the future, not to anticipate trouble,*
> *but to live in the present moment wisely and earnestly."*
> —*Buddha*[87]

You can avoid unnecessary anxiety by not dwelling on the things you cannot control and not fearing things that are not there. Likewise, you can avoid that anxiety by making sure your goal and plan to achieve it are crystal clear. The more gray area there is, the more room for anxiety—which can be crippling for some people.

As mentioned, it takes effort to live a healthy lifestyle. But remaining healthy (and, in turn, best groomed to succeed) also requires rest. Just like our bodies require rest after physical exercise, our minds also need rest after physical exertion, too. Make sure that from time to time you shut off your thoughts and give yourself something peaceful to focus on for a few minutes. Figure out something relaxing for your mind to focus on, because it can otherwise subconsciously choose its own thing to focus on that may make your mind even more exhausted. It's all part of being our healthiest self and preventing ourselves from being overworked, overtired and—ultimately—unproductive.

"True silence is the rest of the mind and is to the spirit what sleep is to the body, nourishment and refreshment."
—William Penn[88]

It's a good practice to begin each day in a positive mindset. This will set the right tone that will carry through your entire day, giving you motivation to move forward on your goal, among other positive benefits. Think positive and inspiring thoughts and surround yourself with positive and inspiring people. It will further attract the like and improve your mental well-being.

If you have a physical ailment, do not let that be a factor in whether you're able to find success or not. Skim through the news and you're likely to see stories of people who, for instance, lost a limb in an accident, but are still able to complete a triathlon. If you listen closely, you'll hear that tons of people are accomplishing things all the time despite any physical setback they have. Why is this? Because their mind is far more powerful than anything they're physically facing—and their mind is telling them, "You can do it!"

> *Consider Shaquem Griffin who was born with a disease that affected his left hand and prevented his fingers from developing. At age 4, his parents witnessed the enormous pain he was experiencing and had his left hand amputated. Despite this, Shaquem insisted he was able to play sports with his twin brother, Shaquill, without his left hand. They competed together in baseball, track and football from children all the way through high school.*

> *Both brothers were such outstanding athletes that they then each received football scholarships and attended and played football for the University of Central Florida.*

> *Shaquem made such an impact that he was named the 2018 Peach Bowl Defensive MVP, American Athletic*

Conference Defensive Player of the Year and was one of two recipients of the 2019 NCAA Inspiration Award, an award presented to current or former NCAA athletes for exceptional, inspirational efforts in dealing with life-altering personal situations.

It doesn't stop there. Amazingly, both brothers were drafted into the NFL. Shaquem landed a place on the Seattle Seahawks.

Shaquem never saw his physical disability as a liability, but rather an inspiration to be the best. By making it to the NFL, he accomplished something that millions of young boys aspire to do, but very few achieve, all with a disability that could have set him back if he had mentally allowed it to. Shaquem proves to be a shining example of how far a person can get, despite all odds, when they maintain a positive mindset.[89]

For those who have a family history of an illness or disease, you might tend to fear it will trickle down to you as well. Don't think like that. Get this—a study out of Johns Hopkins University[90] showed that a positive mindset can truly have an effect on how someone's family medical history can affect them. In the study, those with a family history of heart disease who had a positive outlook on life were one-third as likely compared to their counterparts to have a heart attack or other cardiovascular event within five to 25 years. That's astounding, right?

Even if you're currently battling a disease, having a positive outlook will always benefit you, while having a negative outlook can pose additional mental and physical setbacks along your road to recovery. In essence, you have two choices: Think about your road to recovery with a positive mindset and keep your mind healthy during the journey. Or, think about your road to recovery with a negative mindset, and have your mental well-being suffer as you're battling the disease. The first will, of course, always prove more beneficial for you.

Depending on the severity of a given illness and anticipated outcomes, remaining positive may seem out of the question. For this reason, many health care facilities offer therapy options to patients. If you're suffering from a severe illness, our message to you in this chapter is not to try to mentally overcome the potential negative thoughts you're having on your own, but rather to understand why having a positive outlook will benefit you, and to encourage you to ask for help from a professional to get there if you're struggling.

> *"He who has health has hope; and he who has hope has everything."*
> —*Thomas Carlyle*[91]

For anyone reading this, whether you're currently in a state of positive or negative health, allow this chapter to be a reminder to you that the power of the mind can help you overcome anything your body is facing, and can point you to success. You can achieve anything you set your mind to. If you're battling a physical illness or disability that prevents you from achieving the *exact* thing you originally hoped for, allow your positive mind to guide you to look at your goal and plan to achieve it in a different light. Use it as a benefit! Think bigger. Think brighter. And get out there and get what you want. The healthier you are in mind, the more success you will find in every aspect of life.

CHAPTER 17

Making the Most of Your Time

As you've heard many times throughout this book, our thoughts are the only thing we can completely control. We have complete and total control over whether our thoughts are positive or negative, how we connect with others, how we filter out information, what we focus on, our ability to tap into our creativity, and much more—all thanks to the power of our mind. The power of the mind allows us to dictate our lives. Our minds can not only point us in any direction we choose but can lead us there as well.

Another powerful use of our mind is its ability to help us make the most of the time we have in a given day. While each of us may have a different definition of what "meaningful time" is (which we'll get to in further detail in a few moments), there is a stark difference between how successful people manage time versus how their counterparts manage time.

> *"Don't be fooled by the calendar. There are only as many days in the year as you make use of. One man gets only a week's value out of a year while another man gets a full year's value out of a week."*
> *—Charles Richards*[92]

Successful people are in control of how their time is being spent. They are aware of how much time is needed for certain tasks and activities, and they make a conscious choice about what to spend their time on and when. From their point of view, no time is ever wasted, because they're using it all for a particular purpose, even if that purpose is relaxation or something unrelated to their goal. These individuals have the mental power to look at the period of 24 hours they are allotted each day and mindfully break down how they will spend that time in a manner that's most meaningful to them.

On the other hand, those who are less likely to find success in life are those who believe time controls them. They are of the viewpoint that their tasks and activities are guiding them through life, and there is nothing they can do to change that. These people are those who do not believe they have any power over how their day is being spent—they're only along for the ride.

What happens to the people in the latter category? Often living life in such a way makes these individuals feel unfulfilled. They'll look at all they were hoping to accomplish and realize they didn't accomplish any of it. This is because they never took control over their time to do so.

Control of one's time can and should be taken by each individual if they're hoping to live their most successful life. And it's all done through the power of one's mind.

> *"Life is like a checkerboard and the player opposite you is time.*
> *If you hesitate before moving, or neglect to move promptly,*
> *your men will be wiped off the board by time. You are playing*
> *against a partner who will not tolerate indecision."*
> *—Dr. Napoleon Hill*[93]

Let's rewind just a moment to discuss the concept of "meaningful time." Every person has a different view on what meaningful time is. For some, meaningful time is time spent reading. For others, it may be time spent with his or her family or friends. For some, it can be dedicated relaxation time in front of the television. Because all of us view happiness a bit differently, all of us find happiness in tasks and activities that are different. The one commonality we will stress here in terms of meaningful time, if you're reading this book, should be time spent working toward your goal. We can't reiterate this enough—if you have a goal, you must dedicate time to achieve it or you never will.

The key point we want you to walk away with in the chapter is that, in order to find true success and be as happy as possible with your life, you must determine what meaningful time means for you and take control of the hours in your day to ensure time is being spent appropriately.

We'll pause here, as your brain may have immediately gone to thoughts of your job if you're working at a place you don't love and that doesn't bring you happiness. You may be thinking, "Well, I can't control the hours during my workday. My boss has control over how I spend that time." Yes, that is very true. However, *you* and *only you* have control over whether you remain at that job or not. If you feel controlled by the job, take the control back. If you feel unhappy during the hours spent there—figure out something else you can do that you'll love. Feel trapped there? You're not. There are *always* other options and opportunities for you if you look hard enough and if your mindset about it is positive. We've said it once and we'll say it again: You have one shot at life. Do what makes you happy.

Now let's consider how you might feel if you're currently a student. It's possible you're taking classes that you do not feel are a good use of your time. However, if these are classes you're required to take to finish school—that's just it, they're required. Make the most of them and try to consider what the value in that class might be for you personally. Taking those required classes may also pose an opportunity to network with fellow students and make contacts that will be useful for you in finding success now or down the road. Take some of the lessons you've learned in this book and apply them to accelerate in school and in life. We promise you that there is a benefit to be found in all of the classes you need to take—just look for it!

We all have the same 24 hours in a day. For most, the day is made up of 8 hours of work or school, 8 hours of sleep and 8 hours of spare time. This is a general rule of thumb, though hours can be fluctuated as a person sees appropriate. Some people, for instance, find great benefit in waking up extra early in the morning, as those wee hours when many others are still sleeping pose a great opportunity for them to have quiet, uninterrupted time to spend however they wish. No matter how it's sliced up, we find this method to be a very helpful way of looking at a day and of mentally taking control of the time you have in it.

Depending on what your goal is, time spent working toward that may fall into either the work or spare time category. Either way, as previously discussed, at least some progress should be made each day toward one's goal, so it's essential that it's plotted out somewhere.

While sleep and work/school are self-explanatory, the spare time category will be where meaningful time will be spent very differently from person to person. Just as no one else can dictate what happiness means to you, do not allow outside influences to dictate to you what meaningful time is. If relaxation is an important component for your happiness, then control your time and slot out a time period each day for kicking your feet up and watching a movie, or for quiet mediation, or to go for a long drive— whatever it is that helps you find relaxation. If socializing is meaningful for you, slot out time for lunch with friends. *Only you can determine what is meaningful.*

Will there be some tasks you *have* to do in there that you don't necessarily enjoy? Of course. Maybe it's cooking dinner if you're someone who dislikes cooking. Maybe it's attending a social gathering that you really don't want to attend. Maybe it's writing a paper for school that you've been dreading. There will always be things that come up that you won't find complete happiness in doing, but the key here again is to be in control of that time. Understand what it's being used for. Be aware of it. Plan it out, get the tasks done and move on to the things you enjoy. On the occasion where it's something that you have to do that you don't enjoy, get it over with as soon as possible so you can spend your enjoyment time without having to dwell on it.

Our relative Yvette had three young children when her husband—the financial supporter of the household and the love of her life—suddenly passed away. Not only was she forced to deal with the emotional despair of losing someone she loved so dearly, she was also forced to figure out how the bills would continue to be paid in her husband's absence. She could have let this situation swallow her up, but she did just the opposite. For the sake of herself and her children, she snapped into action to support them. She took a job managing a nearby doctor's office and used this time to figure out what she wanted to accomplish professionally.

Her goal quickly became apparent to her—she wanted to be a nurse. She put her plan into action immediately, beginning to take online courses so that she could maintain her job while still being home on nights and weekends for her children. After receiving her nursing degree, she decided she wanted even more. Today she is a practicing RN who holds a Bachelor of Science degree in nursing (BSN) and is currently pursuing her Master's degree in nursing as a nurse practitioner. She owns a big, beautiful new home and continues to juggle work with helping her now young adult children and caring for her elderly father and her grandson. She manages to do it all and is a model of success to single moms everywhere. Yvette serves as an excellent example of someone who found personal, professional and academic success through her ability to overcome hurdles and excel at time management.

Earlier we mentioned that successful people don't view any time as wasted because they are in control of the hours in their day and why they are spending time on certain things. Let's talk about wasted time. If you're someone who constantly feels like there just aren't enough hours in the day to do all the meaningful things you want to do, we'll once again recommend an audit of how you're using your time. This is a sure-fire way to find wasted time and re-allocate it. Track what you've been spending time on and be specific. Include time spent on things like worrying and procrastination—two things that take up a lot of time in many people's days and that should be eliminated. While everyone will define meaningful time differently—worry, procrastination, and other time drainers we're about to discuss can be universally considered wasted time.

A time-wasting habit people get caught up in is the habit of saying yes to everything. While sometimes a yes is necessary depending on the situation, committing to things that will take up a great deal of your time and pull you away from your goal is an unnecessary habit. There is a difference between doing more than is expected of you and getting to a place where all your spare time is spent on tasks and activities that are insignificant and not meaningful to you. When you're always doing what others want you to do, and not leaving time for anything you want to do, you will generally find yourself in a bad mood. This means you're moving *away* from happiness, instead of toward it.

You'll recall that how you feel about the thought you're thinking or what you are engaged in at the time always tells you whether you are heading in the right direction or not. So, pay attention to how you feel about that time you're spending and make the proper adjustments going forward.

Be honest with yourself as you're auditing your time. The more honest you are, the more you'll be able to easily see where you can cut back. We guarantee there will be areas where you can free up time. Once you free up that time, take control of it and use it meaningfully.

What you may find as you're auditing your time is that there are tasks you're spending time on that can be better done by someone else. It's OK to ask for help! There is no rule written anywhere that says you need to do everything on your own all the time. If there are opportunities to delegate tasks, do it. A great example for those who are parents is asking your children to participate in certain household duties, like helping to clean up after dinner, making beds or straightening up around the house.

If there's a possibility of doing so, seek out people to help you professionally as well—especially if they are more qualified to do the task at hand. Just as it was vital to choose the right people with the right skillsets for your team, it's just as important to make sure you're not wasting a ton of time doing tasks that you're not qualified to do.

Other time-saving tactics include avoiding multitasking (which ends up wasting time, as we've covered), eliminating distractions around you while you're focusing on a meaningful task, excelling at the practice of mentally weeding out unimportant facts, and making decisions quickly and efficiently.

Let's talk about how you tackle your to-do list in a given day as well. Consider what is known as the 80/20 rule.[94] 80 percent of a to-do list will generally be filled with simple, less meaningful tasks. The other 20 percent will generally be filled with more meaningful, though sometimes more difficult, tasks. Those in the latter category can be considered most important and often the ones that will bring you closer to achieving your goal.

Most people will gravitate toward doing the tasks in the 80 percent category first because they are easier. To put yourself miles ahead of most people, look to do the tasks in the 20 percent category first. If you're focused on those bigger and more important tasks first, in cases where nothing else gets accomplished that day at least you'll have crossed off the most meaningful items. And, those 20 percent items will actually get you 80 percent closer to what you want.

So, if you're not already doing so, get those 20 percent tasks to the top of your to-do list and work on them first thing in the morning when you're most energized. Another benefit here is that you will quickly discover that by doing those tasks first, the rest will seem easy and your day will fall into place. This practice also helps you avoid that dreaded wasted time from procrastination on difficult tasks. It also cuts back on worry if those difficult tasks are ones you'd otherwise be worrying and stressing over.

Additionally, as other unpredicted tasks come up throughout your day, get them done right away. Don't wait until right before the deadline to execute on it. This is especially true if the task is something simple. Knock it out right away. Don't even give yourself time to debate when you'll do it. Just get it done.

Likely, as you're practicing the art of taking control of your time, to-do lists and planners will be close friends to you. The trick here in order to not waste any time is to view your to-do lists and schedules in a one-at-a-time manner. For many people reading this, we're sure there have been mornings when you wake up and immediately think, "There is no way I'm going to be able to accomplish everything I need to accomplish today." This is because you're looking at the big picture instead of individual tasks and activities. This leads to you feeling entirely overwhelmed. The worst part is—for many people—they'll freeze up in this state of mind. In order to keep the mind positive and avoid feeling this way (and to avoid wasting time in that frozen zone) focus in on one thing at a time. Cross it off, then move on to the next.

"If you want to make good use of your time, you've got to know what's most important and then give it all you've got."
—*Lee Iacocca*[95]

Also remember that there is no need to do everything perfectly yourself. As you've gone through your auditing exercise, you might see that you're spending far too much time in this area—working on the same task over and over again until you think it's perfect. There's no need! Complete something to the best of your ability. If you're not able to get it exactly right, look for someone else who can help you to get it perfect and move on.

Now that you've became aware of the areas you're likely wasting time, let's remind ourselves that the second component of this is reallocating that time to something meaningful, no matter how you define meaningful time. This is the essence of taking control of your time.

You need to know what you want to use your time for if you expect to be able to use it wisely, just as you need to know what your goal is if you want to be able to develop a solid plan and actually achieve it. Yes, time should be allocated for your goal, but what do you want to use the rest of your time for? Think it through. Be thorough. You'll have time for all of it if you remain in control.

Remember, you can accomplish anything you set your mind to—and we mean anything. Tap into that creativity of yours to come up with some new ideas or projects you want to pursue if you're running out of ideas. Trust us, there will always be something new and exciting you'll want to pursue if you look close enough.

As we know, you can't simply wish for things to happen to you, you have to take action, and everything we've discussed here will be essential in helping you to find the time to take that action. The more you're using your time in a focused manner—to do the things that are most meaningful to you—what you'll find is that you'll need less time than ever to accomplish the things you want to accomplish. Why? Because all of that wasted time you'd been previously spending will be evaporated and refocused toward those meaningful tasks. And having *too much* time will never be a problem for you as a successful person, as you'll always be able to find other meaningful ways to fill it.

> *Our friend recently got surgery in New York City and became fascinated by his surgeon. Our friend was baffled to learn that their surgeon—despite being one of the top-rated in his field in the country, working 70+ hours a week, and helping countless patients a year—was coaching sports teams for his children, serving as chair of multiple local medical boards, volunteering in his community, and training for the New York City marathon.*
>
> *"How could he possibly find time for all of this?" he asked us. And, we knew the answer without having ever spoken a word to this surgeon. The surgeon excelled at the art of controlling his time. For the surgeon, each of the activities mentioned were meaningful to him, and therefore he controlled his time in such a way that he had time for it all. Because he can properly control his time, we're certain the surgeon accomplishes even more than we are aware of.*

Once you've gained control over your time, here is another key tip: Make it a habit. Every time you're about to do something, stop and think about where it falls in your priorities and whether it's a good use of your time or not. Remember that there will always be some things each of us *has* to do, but for the most part we should be able to mentally weed out the meaningful from the unmeaningful—and focus in accordingly. Do this again, and again and again. Soon, you'll realize you're controlling your time without much effort at all. And you'll be accomplishing so much along the way.

As with anything else, be patient with yourself. Habits aren't formed overnight, but once this one is formed, you'll be experiencing an incredible sense of achievement and happiness on a regular basis.

CHAPTER 18

Earning, Budgeting and Investing Money

This chapter is solely focused on money. If you're someone whose goal and definition of success has nothing to do with money, this chapter is not one that is essential for the achievement of your success. That said, we highly recommend that you thoroughly read through this chapter and educate yourself on some of these concepts relevant to money. Whether they are useful for you in the present day or not, we anticipate they will be useful for you at some point in your lifetime.

Let's get into it.

When it comes to money, there are three big topics we like to focus on as they pertain to living your most successful life: Earning, budgeting and investing. We'll begin with earning money.

There are essentially two different ways you can earn money (outside of investing your money, which we'll get to shortly). One is by trading your time for money, or "linear" income. This includes performing a service and getting compensated accordingly. Likewise, if you don't perform the service directly, there is no compensation. There is a great variation in the amount of compensation that one earns on this linear income path, because the bottom line is that you will be paid in life for what you can do that others cannot or do not do.

Here's what we mean by the preceding sentence: A skilled surgeon who is trading his or her time for money can easily make well into six figures and beyond, as they are performing a job that most people do not have the skill or knowledge to do. On the opposite end, someone who is working in the mailroom at a company may be making just a tenth of that surgeon's salary in that same year. This is because, based on skillset and knowledge needed for the mailroom job, most people could do it.

Both of these examples are jobs that trade their time for money, but as we can see, the difference in financial compensation is tremendous. We can clearly see in those examples how the value of a good education and choice of profession plays a big part in your overall financial picture.

> *"An investment in knowledge pays the best interest."*
> *—Benjamin Franklin*[96]

Of course, your chosen profession or career may start off with you trading your time for money in almost any field and can later turn into you owning a business or overseeing others and earning money from their efforts. People who generally make the most money are those who can lead others and inspire others.

If money is something that is important to you, try choosing a career path that offers good compensation for your time (provided of course that it's a career path that will make you happy as well).

The second way of making money (outside of investing) is what is referred to as "residual" income. With this type of income, you do something once and get paid for it over and over again.

A few good examples of this are:

- developing or finding a new use for technology, like Amazon and Uber
- coming up with an invention, patenting it and receiving royalties
- real estate investing

- writing a book or a song
- leading sales organizations

As you can see, most of the higher-paying linear income fields require much traditional education but can certainly be worthwhile, especially if you can grow into a leadership position. On the residual income end, income opportunities are certainly more entrepreneurial and take time to turn a profit but can also be worthwhile. In most of these cases, you will work hard with little or no compensation at the beginning, but eventually get paid without having to participate. There is no right answer on what direction that you choose to earn your money, it's a personal choice and—as with anything else we've reviewed in this book—it should all be about what makes you happy.

Now let's talk about budgeting money. Just as many people go through life not realizing the power they have to take control of their time, many people live their life in the same manner when it comes to their money. These people may go through life with a focus on collecting a paycheck simply to pay their bills. This leaves them regularly feeling as though money controls them. Many times, this then also results in these individuals being trapped in jobs they dislike for years and years—because in their mind—that paycheck dictates their life.

Well, let us assure you, it does not have to work that way. Each of us can have control over our money if we choose to. All we need to do is understand the importance of money management.

> *"Those who don't manage their money will always work for those who do."*
> *—Dave Ramsey*[97]

You control your money; your money does not control you. If you feel as though money is currently controlling you, an easy way to take back that control is to do an audit, similar to what we did for time. Sit down with your list of monthly bills and your bank statement and figure out where your money is really going. While everyone's financial situation will be different, we can guarantee that if this isn't an exercise you've done before, you will always find one or more areas where you're spending money unnecessarily. Trim that out. Don't spend beyond your means, and you won't have to worry about living paycheck to paycheck.

Once you've looked at where you're spending your money and are able to free up extra dollars, bank it. Come up with a plan for how you'll continue to cut back in coming months and use that extra money more meaningfully. If you're struggling, don't be afraid to ask for help from a financial advisor or a friend or family member who is good at budgeting. They can help point you in the right direction so that you're in control of your own money. Watch how your happiness will increase immediately as stress of financial woes is lifted off your shoulders.

A simple practice when budgeting money is to save 10 percent right off the top from each paycheck for savings/investments. Then, use the next 10 percent to pay down the principle on any debt you may have. The remaining 80 percent should be used to live off. If you happen to be temporarily struggling financially, it may sound difficult to live on the 80 percent when you're having a hard time living on 100 percent right now. However, we assure you it can be done. What it may require in the short-term is a willingness to take on overtime hours or a side job to make a little extra cash. Within a short time, your savings will build, your debt will be reduced and you will begin to not worry anymore. This will clear your mind to move forward toward your goal and happiness.

Our relative, Jim, has a practice he uses that he swears by. If he wants to buy something, he saves his money and buys it using cash only. If he wants new furniture: He pays cash.

If he wants a nice vacation: He pays cash. If he wants a new car: He pays cash. He even bought his new home with cash. What a great personal financial policy! Imagine the peace of mind he has when it comes to finances knowing that he never has to pay interest on any of those things. In addition to his ability to save for the things he wants to purchase, he saves the remaining of his extra salary or invests it, as appropriate. He is debt free and living with the ultimate peace of mind.

There is an excellent book on managing your money, told through a collection of parables set 8,000 years ago in ancient Babylon, entitled *The Richest Man in Babylon* by George S. Clason. We would highly recommend it, as it contains some life-changing tips and stories that may change your financial future.

Always remember to remain positive about your financial state. If it's bad now, it will get better. If your mind knows that to be true, it will be true.

Now that we've covered some thoughts on managing money, let's quickly cover *feelings* about money. Some people have been subconsciously trained throughout their lifetime to feel negatively about money. Maybe they grew up in a household where money was always very scarce, so they were taught from a young age that money was evil—it was something that was always coveted but never had, and it was unfair that others had money and they did not. If this—or something similar—seems familiar to you in your life, it's time to change your mind-set about money, otherwise it will be difficult to ever have a positive experience with it. While some would say money is the root of all evil, in actuality it can be a big part of happiness.

As the saying goes, money can't buy happiness. While we certainly agree to an extent, the sheer *lack* of money can certainly lead to unhappiness. This is because if you're unable to pay your bills or put food on the table, it's going to directly lead you to a life filled with stress, anxiety and, ultimately, unhappiness. Oppositely, having money can mean being able to do what you want in life, and acquire the things you want without financial constraints.

And while money can't buy happiness, money can buy freedom. It can buy freedom to do what you want, when you want to do it. It can buy freedom from financial stress and debt and freedom to—at your own discretion—reward yourself and those around you. Most importantly, money can offer you the financial freedom to pursue a job that will make you happy, without having to worry about keeping a job you're unhappy with simply to pay your bills.

Ultimately, you should feel good about money. If you find that you feel guilty in any way once you've acquired money, consider going back to our earlier habit of doing more than is expected of you—and translating that to giving financially to those who are in need. Your generosity will make them feel good, and you feel good about the use of that money as well.

Finally, when it comes to money, let's discuss investing. There is almost no better feeling when it comes to money than having your money work for you.

> *"It's not how much money you make, but how much money you keep, how hard it works for you, and how many generations you keep it for."*
> *—Robert Kiyosaki*[98]

In our discussion about budgeting money, we recommended taking 10 percent off the top of your paycheck for investing purposes. Over time that can turn into a small fortune for you, provided you make the right investment. Whether you're looking to invest in real estate, stocks, bonds, commodities, mutual funds or something else, we advise you seek the proper financial counsel if you are not an expert in the given field. This expert can match up your financial goals with the proper investments.

> *For five* **years, our relative, Danny,** *budgeted properly and invested more than 50* **percent** *of his income into real estate ventures. Today those investments are worth three times what he initially invested. Talk about good budgeting and making your money work for you, it's perfect!*

As we are not investment advisors, we don't want to delve into all the different facets of investing, but in addition to seeking a financial advisor, there are also many good books and publications that can be of assistance to you in this matter.

While money isn't everything, it can certainly be of help to you in living a comfortable life—whether your goal has to do with business or not. With money, you can live in a better home in a better neighborhood. You can drive a better car, you and your children can go to better schools, you can afford better colleges, you can afford better health care and you can go on better vacations. Most importantly, it provides you with peace of mind regarding financial matters, gives you time to focus on bigger and better things and provides you with the opportunity to give back/donate to help those less fortunate. It's certainly not everything, but it can be a big part of living a successful and happier life.

CHAPTER 19

Practicing the Right Habits

All of the lessons we have covered in this book are essentially habits that, when practiced in your life, can help guide you to living your most successful life possible. All of the lessons we've covered should become habits in your life in order for you to live a more successful life both now and in the future. Our habits, whether good or bad, can dictate our lives just as our thoughts and attitudes can. By taking control of our habits through thought, we can ensure we are the ones dictating how our lives go, not the other way around.

Just as with anything else, if our habits are positive, we can expect positive results. If our habits our negative, we can expect negative results. It's as simple as that.

If you're someone who makes it a habit of remaining positive and motivated toward achieving your goal, you're enhancing your odds of achieving it. If you're someone who makes it a habit of worrying that you will fail at achieving your goal, you likely will.

> *"Whether you think you can, or you think you can't, you're right."*
> *—Henry Ford*[99]

Repeated thoughts and actions you implore in your everyday life eventually become a habit. We're sure you've noticed that to be true in your lifetime. The more you think and act on something, the more of a fixed habit it will become. It is all thanks to the Forces of Natures that are at play. They are always working, no matter what.

These Forces of Nature can work to establish your habits without you even realizing it. However, we have the ability to change those habits if we desire and let the Forces of Nature work their power to help us in establishing the right habits.

On a positive note, because you have control over your own habits through thought, if you're aware of the thoughts you're thinking you can set yourself in any direction you choose. The key here is using your willpower to take control and maintain that control. On a negative note, if you're not mindful of the Forces of Nature and their constant work, they can begin to take control of you and take you in any direction *they* choose. The latter is not a way to live a successful life, as you can imagine. Let the Forces of Nature work *for you* … not *against you.*

> *"We are what we repeatedly do. Excellence, then, is not an*
> *act, but a habit."*
> *—Will Durant*[100]

Because the Forces of Natures will control whatever they are able to control, certain things around us become predictable. If it's raining outside and the temperature drops low enough, it will change to snow. Nothing is there to control this environmental habit aside from the Forces of Nature. The snow has no choice but to form.

Here is where you have a choice in the matter: If that snow has accumulated on your car's windshield and you need to run an errand, based on the habits you've followed in the past, you're going to clear your windshield of the snow before you begin driving. You do not *have* to do this, but because you've chosen to do it time and time again, and it has helped you to drive safely, you'll choose to do it again. That's part of the Forces of Nature as well.

See, while certain things working in the universe are out of our own control, including habits of nature and habits of others around us—what is *always* available for each of us to individually control is how we think and what we do. We control our own habits, not anyone else—and we do so through controlled thought. The trick, again, is realizing that we have the ability to take that control... and then doing it!

It's possible that, prior to reading this book, you've thought little about the habits you currently have. Let us assure you, you have plenty. Stop here for a few moments and consider them. Wiping your windshield of snow before you drive a car is something you likely learned very early on in life by seeing others do it, and then you began doing it as needed, once you began driving. The more you repeat it, the more it becomes a habit. Do you start your day with a cup of coffee? Do you put on shoes before you leave the house? Do you wear a jacket if it's cold outside? Pay attention closely and you'll realize that many things you're doing each day are out of habit. You've repeated them so many times, that now you do them without even realizing.

It's the same for the more important mental habits in your life. The habit of expecting good or bad outcomes to situations in life can mean all the difference in those actual outcomes.

Now, as you're mentally going through some examples of habits you may have, consider if any are particularly detrimental. One to fully consider, especially after having made it nearly to the end of this book, is if any of your previously-existing habits are working against the success lessons we've discussed. Once again, all of the lessons we've covered should become habits if you want to achieve success with your goal, and continue that stream of success for the remainder of your life.

Let's recap the habits here again for a moment:

- Live your happiest life.
- Change your limiting beliefs.
- Create a positive mindset.
- Define your goal and plan to achieve it.
- Build your inner faith.
- Do more than is expected of you.
- Remain motivated.
- Maintain and control your enthusiasm.
- Exercise self-discipline.
- Surround yourself with the right people.
- Excel at the art of connecting with others.
- Separate fact from opinion.
- Remain focused.
- Use hurdles to your advantage.
- Tap into your creativity.
- Focus on your health.
- Control your time.
- Earn, budget and invest money.

Check in on yourself here. Think closely about how you're doing with all these things. Have you forgotten to begin implementing any of them? Be truthful and patient with yourself, but also realize that all these tactics are both helpful and necessary to living a more successful life.

Those success tactics are the foundation for the *right habits* you should be practicing day in and day out. You should be repeating them over and over and over, as relevant. The more you repeat a habit, the more intense it will become, just as the more you think a positive thought, the more positive the outcome will be.

You see how all of this is connected? You see how important it is to take control of your own mind, your own thoughts and your own habits? You have the willpower to do it all—so do it!

Your personal willpower plays a very big role in this process. You must exercise it, especially in cases where you're starting a new habit or attempting to change an existing one. Your willpower will push you through—as long as you allow it to. With your willpower backing you, no habit will be impossible to start, stop or alter. Any negative circumstance you may be facing will be able to be overcome through your personal willpower to do so. You'll come out on top and winning will become a habit.

When we first talked about establishing your goal and plan to achieve it, we addressed the fact that both of those need to be as specific as possible. Same goes for any habit you are working on. Be specific! Imagine how you will feel once you've put these habits to work for you and you're inching toward accomplishing your goal. Imagine how you'll feel once this habit leads you directly to the very thing you want out of life. It feels great, right? Think about it and feel it, again and again. Put the power of this law of nature on your side heading toward your goal and you will be amazed at the results.

> *"What this power is I cannot say; all I know is that it exists and it becomes available only when a man is in that state of mind in which he knows exactly what he wants and is fully determined not to quit until he finds it."*
> *—Alexander Graham Bell*[101]

Here's something you may be wondering: What if you've successfully established a habit and then realize it's no longer working for you? Change it. It's as simple as that, with your willpower on your side. We've said many times that, while being specific and deliberate with your plan to achieve your goal is critical, you must also be willing to make any necessary changes as needed throughout the process. Things aren't always going to go exactly as you anticipated, so we absolutely must be flexible at those points in time. The very same goes for habits. Make them specific and repetitious and be willing to be flexible as needed.

How do you know if a habit is *right?* When it comes to success, if the habit is going against any of the positive success habits we've reviewed in this book, take that as a sign that it is not right. Likewise, if it's something we haven't covered here, remember that how you *feel* about a thought you're having can help guide you as to whether it's sending you in the right or wrong direction… same goes for habits as well. Listen to how you're feeling about it and go from there. Trust yourself. You've already shown by reading this book that you're ready for success. You're going to get yourself there, without a doubt.

> *"I learned to be with myself, rather than avoiding myself with limiting habits; I started to be aware of my feelings more, rather than trying to numb them."*
> *—Judith Wright*[102]

We'll give you an example of a negative habit that prevents millions of people every single day from living a successful life and that is the habit of worrying about what other people think. This habit has so many negative effects that we could fill an entire book on this topic alone. Ultimately, this negative habit can be detrimental to someone's mind, body and soul. We cannot say this enough: Stop worrying about what everyone else thinks. What they think has nothing to do with your happiness unless you let it. You are in control.

Not everyone in this world is out to get you, as you may have allowed yourself to envision in your mind at certain times in life. The honest truth is that most people are not even thinking about you or what you're doing— they're focused on themselves. You should be too! Stop letting this take up space in your mind. If this is a habit you currently have, break it as soon as possible.

Just as nothing is impossible to achieve, no negative habit is impossible to change. As you're realizing habits you have that are not right—whether those are setting you back in terms of success, or negatively affecting you in another way—use your thoughts to help you to break that habit and replace it with a new one. There are so many great things you can be spending your time and mind-space on, so focus on those instead.

In Chapter 3 of this book, where we discussed creating a positive mind-set, we equated your thoughts to a fork in a flowing river, where one side flowed positive thoughts and the other negative thoughts. We reviewed how to begin diverting little by little that negative flow to the positive flow side. The same applies here to your habits—a slight change of thought, then a slight action behind that thought, starts to change the bad habit to good. Then, as you repeat that thought and action, a new good habit begins to form, and eventually takes over and becomes the norm.

You will be amazed at the result of changing habits, especially as they apply to your thoughts. The simple habit of waking up in the morning and writing down what you are grateful for, appreciating the day that lies before you and expecting it to yield good results for you, will change your life.

Remember, at the end of the day—you are in control of your thoughts. This means you are also in control of your habits. *Complete and total control.* Never forget that. It's the most important lesson from this entire book: You are in control of what happens in your life.

CHAPTER 20

Final Thoughts: Being Patient with Yourself

Now that you've reached the end of the book, take a moment to consider all the information you've just absorbed. We know there is a lot to consider here—and many things we're asking you to practice routinely in order to live a more successful life. The beauty is, upon practicing these habits again and again, this will all slowly begin to become second nature to you. These practices will literally become habitual. Before you know it, success—and happiness along the way—will be the *only option*. You'll be looking for it constantly. You'll be expecting it at every turn. And it will be there waiting for you.

Some of you may have found the lessons in this book to be things you're already familiar with. Maybe you've encountered one or more of these similar lessons elsewhere, and maybe you've even been practicing some of these lessons for a while based on your previous knowledge. For others, all of this may be brand new to you, so right now—especially if you've read through this book quickly—it may seem like you're about to embark on an uphill battle. Let us assure you here, you are not. These lessons are surprisingly simple to begin to incorporate, especially if you don't allow yourself to overthink them. Consider one lesson at a time. Master them slowly but surely. Think of this not as a sprint, but rather as a life-long marathon.

Revisit the chapters in this book that were of most interest or relevance to you. Then, revisit them again. Break out a highlighter and highlight key parts. Be patient with yourself throughout the process. Reread this book many times. As you grow and your perspective on life changes, you will always find new things to learn from this book that you hadn't seen before. Rereading the book will also help further reinforce what you already know. We encourage you to become a life-long student of success and happiness.

As with anything, if this is all new to you, it's going to take time. Don't stress yourself out. Remember in Chapter 1 how we discussed how necessary it is to find happiness along the way to success? Think of that often. If you're allowing yourself to feel overwhelmed and stressed about the way you view this practice, sooner or later you're going to be tempted to throw in the towel. And, we don't want that! It's your life—and you have the complete and total power to make it the happiest and most successful it can be. It's in your hands, if you choose to take the reins.

> *"At the end of the day, you are in control of your own happiness. Life is going to happen whether you overthink it, overstress it or not. Just experience life and be happy along the way. You can't control everything in your life, but you can control your happiness."*
> *—Holly Holm*[103]

Each of us is only human. We will make mistakes or miss deadlines or encounter problems we can't seem to find a solution for. We will find ourselves overthinking situations that we should have instead let slide past us, or forgetting to show gratitude, or neglecting to go above and beyond—it's all part of human nature. No one is perfect, and we—by no means—are asking you to be so. We encourage you to strive to achieve what you want out of life while having fun and enjoying the process.

This practice of living a more successful life is also about knowing what to do *after* we encounter a slipup, and that is to persevere and keep moving forward. It's only by doing so that you will be able to find success again and again throughout your life. Never give up, and you'll be thankful you hadn't, each and every time. Don't allow hurdles of any kind to get you down on yourself or let your mind skew negative. Instead, come to terms with the situation, look for the benefit, and then immediately move on from it.

> *"Remember that setbacks are only challenges in disguise. Look at them as lessons and don't waste time beating yourself up. Just get back on track and focus on what you want. It's up to you, and you will do it!"*
> —*Jorge Cruise*[104]

Keep going. Keep reviewing the lessons. Despite any hurdles, setbacks and/or criticism from others around you, and despite the times you get into your own head thinking, "This is way too much for me" or "There is no way I can devote enough time to all of this." Despite *all of that*—you can and will be successful in whatever manner you define success as long as you take the time to incorporate these lessons into your life.

> *"The secret of getting ahead is getting started. The secret to getting started is breaking down your overwhelming tasks into small manageable tasks, and then starting on the first one."*
> —*Mark Twain*[105]

Remember, in those times when you're feeling behind the ball, success does not come easy. You have to work for it. It takes both time and effort, and therefore, you must be patient. Will it always be easier to give up? Absolutely! But, if you're committed to living the happiest and most successful life you can live, then not giving up will prove to be incredibly beneficial for you. Your wildest dreams are going to be realized—as long as you're willing to put in the work to achieve them and be patient along the way.

> *"Patience and fortitude conquer all things."*
> *—Ralph Waldo Emerson*[106]

Keep the momentum going as much as you possibly can. Once your goal and plan to achieve it are clearly defined, hit the ground running as soon as possible. We've spoken at length about staying motivated and enthused, and we know that to keep it going we have to be excited about what it is we're doing. If you're losing that feeling of excitement, revisit this book. Allow it to help guide you in understanding what is and isn't working for you. Again, this is all about *you* and what will make *you* feel happy. Your personal happiness and success can only be defined by you and you alone.

Be flexible. Be persistent. Once these practices become habitual, you'll begin to notice how you're living your life differently than ever before. The sun will seem to be shining for you, even on days when it's pouring rain. Things will naturally be going your way because your mind believes and expects they will, without any conscious effort on your part to believe so. Succeeding and winning will become second nature for you.

Once you've achieved your goal—whether you defined it as something short-term or long-term—here's what is likely to happen: You're going to be so impressed with yourself and your ability to apply these lessons that you're going to want to do it again to achieve something else. It will be addictive! It'll be encouraging to see how you've made such progress and you'll wonder what else you can apply this practice to.

The adventure of life never ends for those who practice these lessons. When you get what you want, you'll want something else.

Let us remind you that you can apply everything you've learned in this book to *anything* you want to achieve in life. It will work every time. As long as you believe it is possible, put in the time and effort with a positive mindset, and are willing to be patient with yourself and the process, anything can and will be yours.

What if you fall off track? What if an entire week, or month or year passes, and you haven't taken a step toward achieving what you want out of life? That's OK—start today. Your goal is just that... it's *yours.* Only you can say when you're mentally ready to begin taking steps to achieve it. And it's never too late to go out there and get what it is that you want. Our best advice is to act now. If you wait for everything to be perfect to take action on your goal, you could find yourself waiting seemingly forever, and wind up *never* taking action. Don't allow yourself to feel guilty (you'll recall that guilt takes up a lot of unwanted negative space in your mind) and instead let a feeling of excitement overcome you as you prepare to take your first step in your journey. Success is right at your fingertips!

If there are parts of this book that you're struggling with, simply revisit them. If you feel as though you need a deeper dive into any of the lessons here—or the practice of living a more successful life as a whole—consider purchasing our supplementary Action Steps Manual that we've developed that walks you through each of these chapters over the course of 20 weeks. The pace of the Action Steps Manual allows you to fully absorb all the lessons by writing and taking action for each lesson, at a speed that may feel more comfortable to you.

For our Action Steps Manual please visit www.SuccessCornerstone.com.

If you find you are implementing all these habits and are not moving any closer to your goal over time, there could be a limiting belief in place that is holding you back. At that point, we would highly recommend revisiting Chapter 2 of this book and doing in-depth self-reflection. If you uncover a limiting belief that is holding you back, do as we suggested and begin to erase it and replace with a new, positive belief. As we've mentioned, our gratitude exercise is an excellent way to begin to move that needle.

Just by finishing this book and applying even some of the habits found here, you have already done more than most in moving toward what you want in life. There are now strong connections that have formed—that between us, between you and others who are reading this book, between you and success and between you and happiness as you define it. Make the most of it. Enjoy your life and have fun.

You now have the knowledge to begin to change the course of your life and potentially the lives of future generations. We have one shot at life and we encourage you to do something meaningful with yours. Accomplish what makes you happy. If you were born and raised in undesirable circumstances, be the one who changes the path for your family and sets an example for future generations to come.

> *We first met Jeff and Lindsey on a business trip to Florida to preview apartment buildings for sale. Jeff was the assistant on-site manager of a blighted, bank-foreclosed, 46-unit complex. Jeff, Lindsey and their children were living in a tiny two-bedroom apartment in a marginal neighborhood rent-free in exchange for Jeff doing maintenance and handling tenant problems for the bank. Aside from the free rent, Jeff was not being paid. He was a contractor by trade and it was late 2009 when there was no construction activity happening in the area. There was no real work to be found anywhere for him and their only vehicle was an old broken-down truck. Their young children were not yet school aged so Lindsey stayed home with them while Jeff would try to find anything to bring home a couple of dollars for the family. At times, Jeff would have to give blood just to get enough money to buy food for the family.*

Our company wound up purchasing this building a couple of months later and hired Jeff and Lindsey to help us run it. Working for us, they received the same rent-free apartment and were now being paid as well. They didn't just help us run it, however. In a very short time, they took over. They did such an outstanding job turning the project around that we acquired more properties in the same area for them to run… then more and more.

Today Jeff and Lindsey still work with us but now in a management capacity. They no longer live in that apartment because now they own their own beautiful home. They no longer have that old broken-down truck and now they have two nice vehicles in the driveway. They also have a landscaping business on the side and are now saving up to buy an even larger home. We learned from Jeff not long ago that he was the first person ever in his family to own their own home.

We tell you this story to remind you of this: Don't spend time comparing yourself to where others are in life, because it's not how far up the ladder of success you are, but how many rungs you have climbed that makes the ultimate difference.

You now have the ability through the knowledge you have gained in this book to break the chains that may have been holding you back. You have the ability to overcome any mental conditioning you may have previously had. It's completely in your power to break those imaginary chains.

Consider this particular practice that was used for hundreds of years at the circus when elephants were one of the dominant features. When the elephant was just a baby, they would tie one leg with a chain to a stake in the ground to keep the elephant from running away. At first the baby elephant would pull and pull to try and free itself to no avail. It was simply too small and weak. In a short period of time it became conditioned to believe that it could not free itself from the chain. As the elephant grew and became a full-grown adult—easily capable of pulling the stake out of the ground and freeing itself—it never even tried, as it was mentally conditioned to believe it was unable to free itself.

Many people are slaves to the same mental conditioning, believing they are tied to their stake and there is nothing they can do about it. You know better now. Just pull out the stake and move on to what is going to make you happy in your life. Don't concern yourself with what others think, do or say. This is your life. Make the most of it. Live it the way you want. That's real success.

Remember, you have the power to deliberately create the life you choose. Stay focused on what it is that you want, believe it to be possible in your mind and then take action toward it.

If you are contemplating a goal and path and are not sure which way to go, always remember to pay attention to how you feel about the thoughts you're having—the one that makes you feel good and sends a chill down your spine is always the correct thought and the direction to head in. Trust that thought.

Everything we've discussed in this book is a life-long practice. This isn't something you should practice once until you achieve your goal, and then put it behind you. This is a way of life. A way of thinking. A way of being.

We hope you have found these lessons useful and that you begin to implement them into your own life, if you haven't already, to achieve whatever it is that you desire to achieve, whether it's a personal goal, a professional goal or an academic goal. Through these lessons you've now been provided with *The Foundation of a Successful Life*—now build on it; anything is possible with these habits put into place—and we mean *anything*!

APPENDIX

Throughout *The Foundation of a Successful Life* we've included plenty of lessons for you to practice. Below are some of the most vital lessons you'll want to practice on a daily, monthly, annual and as-needed basis.

Daily:

1. **Write in Your Gratitude Journal**

   Your gratitude journal should be written in once per day, ideally in the morning to get your mind immediately flowing in a positive direction. In addition to writing five things you are grateful for that day, you may also wish to write five things you *will* be grateful for once you have achieved them, as if you already have them. (For example, if your goal is to become president at your company, you might write down, "I am grateful that I am president of my company.")

2. **Use a Day Planner**

   A day planner helps keep you organized, deadline-driven and disciplined. Referring to your planner and keeping it up-to-date will help you prioritize deliverables and remain focused on achieving your goal. As you are working toward your goal, try to cross off at least one item per day that fulfills your plan to achieve your goal.

3. **Focus on Your Vision Board**

   Once you've created a vision board, you should keep it in a prominent place in your home or office – somewhere you'll be sure to see it regularly. At all times you should have your mind preoccupied with what you want, and taking time here and there throughout your day to glance at your vision board will help you in that mission. Your vision board will help you clearly visualize the life you want… and get it!

4. **Do More Than is Expected of You**

   Whether it's helping someone else through an act of kindness or doing something extra to benefit you and your personal/professional/academic life, every day you should be striving to do more than is expected of you in situations. Need a refresher on what this means? Flip back to Chapter 6 for the complete rundown.

Monthly:

1. **Revisit Your Happiness List and Act on It**

   As noted in Chapter 1, the initial happiness list you make is likely going to change over time. What makes you happy in this very moment may not be the same thing that makes you happy in several months from now. We recommend revisiting your happiness list once a month to see if there is anything you want to add or remove from it.

   Likewise, you should try to act on your happiness list at least once a month as well by doing or moving toward one of the things that makes you feel happy. Why? Because happiness is something that should be experienced along a person's path to success, so allowing yourself to experience it regularly will make for a far better life.

2. **Evaluate Your Plan and Brainstorm**

Slight revisions to your plan to achieve your goal may be required more frequently than on a monthly basis, but at least once per month you should spend a bit of time evaluating your plan and your progress against it. Determine whether the plan is working as intended, and if not, tweak your plan accordingly.

This may also serve as a good opportunity for some brainstorming, if needed. Remember to fully dedicate yourself/your mind to your brainstorm session as recommended in the book and clear the room of any distractions. Then, ask yourself the right questions, such as, "What is the answer to…?" or, "How do I…?".

If you find that progress on your plan is lacking, you may try bringing in the reward system we recommended. Look at your plan, identify key milestone points and promise yourself a reward of some kind (can be either small or big) once that milestone is reached. This can serve as a very helpful motivator.

Annually:

1. **Assess Your Team**

If your goal is specifically a professional one and requires a team of experts to achieve, it's a good practice to evaluate on an annual basis how the team is working together. Ultimately, your team should collectively be working together to further strengthen each other's strengths, delegate weaknesses and stay focused on what it is that each of you are particularly good at. Your team's strengths should allow you to collectively accomplish the goal. If a member (or multiple) of the team are not working out, it is OK – and in most cases necessary – to remove them as the process moves forward and replace them with someone else who is a better fit. Ongoing harmony is most important, so changing group members is sometimes inevitable.

As Needed:

1. **Look for the Silver Lining in All Negative Circumstances**

   A big part of what you've learned in the book is to examine every negative situation and find the positive in it. In every hurdle an advantage can be found if you look hard enough. As negative situations arise, remember to be on the lookout for what the benefit in the situation may be. Sometimes it may take some time to see it, but it is there. Keep asking the question, "Where is the benefit in this?" Sooner or later it will show up, provided you keep asking the question and expecting the answer.

2. **Hype Yourself Up Through a Song or Reading**

   When you feel motivation is lacking, remember to try listening to one of your favorite songs to help get that fuel flowing again. Likewise, motivation can be sparked by referring to your favorite part of this book or another inspirational passage. Have the passages highlighted and on-hand for when you need a boost. Then flip to them and re-read them again until your mind is back to a motivated state.

CITATIONS

1: Feloni, R. (2015, June 25). KFC founder Colonel Sanders didn't achieve his remarkable rise to success until his 60s. Retrieved from https://www.businessinsider.com/how-kfc-founder-colonel-sanders-achieved-success-in-his-60s-2015-6

2: Happiness. In *The Merriam-Webster.com Dictionary.* Retrieved from https://www.merriam-webster.com/dictionary/happiness

3: Audrey Hepburn Quotes. Retrieved from https://www.brainyquote.com/quotes/audrey_hepburn_413489

4. Rowling, J. K. (2008, June 5). Text of J.K. Rowling Speech. Retrieved from https://news.harvard.edu/gazette/story/2008/06/text-of-j-k-rowling-speech/

5: A Quote by Abraham Lincoln. Retrieved from https://www.goodreads.com/quotes/69-folks-are-usually-about-as-happy-as-they-make-their

6: Dale Carnegie Quotes. Retrieved from https://www.brainyquote.com/quotes/dale_carnegie_140941

7: The Feeling of Clay in Your Hands. (2017, October 23). Retrieved from http://readjoyce.com/uncategorized/2368/

8. Success Staff. (2019, January 21). 15 Quotes to Overcome Your Self-Limiting Beliefs. Retrieved from https://www.success.com/15-quotes-to-overcome-your-self-limiting-beliefs/

9. Byrne, R. (2010). *The Power.* New York, NY: Atria Books.

10: Hill, N. (2016, August 2). *Napoleon Hill's Master Key* [Motion picture]. United States: Cine-O-Matic, Inc.

11: Nightingale, E. (2016, November 18). *Strangest Secret Library.* Lulu.com

12: Peale, N.V. (2019, March 18). *The Power of Positive Thinking.* Samaira Book Publishers.

13: 50 Cent. (2019, August 15). Retrieved from https://www.biography.com/ musician/50-cent

14: Richard M. DeVos Quotes. Retrieved from https://www.brainyquote.com/ quotes/richard_m_devos_955477

15: Zig Ziglar Quotes. Retrieved from https://www.brainyquote.com/quotes/ zig_ziglar_617769

16: Economy, P. (2019, February 19). 50 Inspirational Quotes to Motivate You to Get Out There and Get It Done. Retrieved from https://www.inc.com/peter-economy/50 -inspirational-quotes-to-motivate-you-to-get-out-there-get-it-done.html

17: Davidson, J. (2016, September 26). Attitudes, Not Aptitudes, Control Our Lives in Full. Retrieved from http://clevelandbanner.com/stories/attitudes-not-aptitudes -control-our-lives-in-full,43268

18: A Quote from Think and Grow Rich. Retrieved from https://www.goodreads. com/quotes/77253-whatever-the-mind-can-conceive-and-believe-it-can-achieve

19: Walt Disney Quotes. Retrieved from https://www.brainyquote.com/quotes/ walt_disney_163027

20: Ralph Waldo Emerson Quotes. Retrieved from https://www.brainyquote.com/ quotes/ralph_waldo_emerson_108797

21: A Quote from The Light in the Heart. Retrieved from https://www.goodreads. com/quotes/7859382-take-responsibility-of-your-own-happiness-never-put-it-in

22: Edison Failed 10,000 Times Before Perfecting the Incandescent Electric Light Bulb. (2017, March 20). Retrieved from http://www.naphill.org/tftd/ thought_for_the_day_monday_march_20_2017/

23: Rollins, K. (2018, May 30). What Is the Origin of LeBron James's "Chosen 1" Tattoo? Retrieved from https://www.si.com/nba/2018/05/30/origin-lebron-james -chosen-1-tattoo

24: Norman Vincent Peale Quotes. Retrieved from https://www.brainyquote.com/ quotes/norman_vincent_peale_132560?src=t_believe_in_yourself

25: A Quote by Napoleon Hill. Retrieved from https://www.goodreads.com/quotes/509939-desire-backed-by-faith-knows-no-such-word-as-impossible

26: Emile Coue Quotes. Retrieved from https://www.brainyquote.com/quotes/emile_coue_127527

27: George Burns Quotes. Retrieved from https://www.brainyquote.com/quotes/george_burns_103932

28: T.P.'s Weekly: Volume 10. (1907, December 31). Retrieved from https://play.google.com/store/books/details?id=7phFAQAAMAAJ&rdid=book-7phFAQAAMAAJ&rdot=1

29. Latson, J. (2014, October 21). How Edison Invented the Light Bulb - And Lots of Myths About Himself. Retrieved from https://time.com/3517011/thomas-edison/

30: Brad Henry Quotes. Retrieved from https://www.brainyquote.com/quotes/brad_henry_167807

31: Gary Ryan Blair Quotes. Retrieved from https://www.brainyquote.com/quotes/gary_ryan_blair_125852

32: Dyer, W.W. (2002, September 1). *It's Never Crowded Along the Extra Mile.* Hay House.

33: Ross Mathews Quotes. Retrieved from https://www.brainyquote.com/quotes/ross_mathews_644683

34: Berman, N. (2018, June 11). 10 Things You Didn't Know About Walmart CEO Doug McMillon. Retrieved from https://moneyinc.com/walmart-ceo-doug-mcmillon/

35: World Class Advisors. Napoleon Hill Principle 5: Go the Extra Mile. Retrieved from http://worldclassadvisors.com/pdf/napoleon_hill_principle_5.pdf

36: Booker T. Washington Quotes. Retrieved from https://www.brainyquote.com/quotes/booker_t_washington_382202

37: Theodore Roosevelt Quotes. Retrieved from https://www.brainyquote.com/quotes/theodore_roosevelt_163580

38: Orlando Aloysius Battista Quotes. Retrieved from https://www.azquotes.com/quote/871455

39: The Editors of Encyclopaedia Britannica. Alberto R. Gonzales United States official. Retrieved from https://www.britannica.com/biography/Alberto-R-Gonzales

40: Henry Ford Quotes. Retrieved from https://www.brainyquote.com/quotes/henry_ford_101486

41: Hill, N. (1997, October 1). *Napoleon Hill's Keys to Success: The 17 Principles of Personal Achievement.* TarcherPerigee.

42: Mario Andretti Quotes. Retrieved from https://www.brainyquote.com/quotes/mario_andretti_130613

43: Mandino, O. (1997, January 1). *The Greatest Secret in the World.* Bantam.

44: Super Bowl History. Retrieved from https://www.pro-football-reference.com/super-bowl/

45: Mary Kay Ash Quotes. Retrieved from https://www.brainyquote.com/quotes/mary_kay_ash_386553

46: There is Real Magic in Enthusiasm. Retrieved from https://quotes.yourdictionary.com/author/quote/557200

47: Ralph Waldo Emerson Quotes. Retrieved from https://www.brainyquote.com/quotes/ralph_waldo_emerson_134859

48: Vince Lombardi Quotes. Retrieved from https://www.brainyquote.com/quotes/vince_lombardi_402267

49: Grenville Kleiser Quotes. Retrieved from https://www.brainyquote.com/quotes/grenville_kleiser_158311

50: Kalla, S. (2015, January 18). Keys to Excellence (Even Michael Jordan Had to Do It). Retrieved from https://www.forbes.com/sites/susankalla/2012/05/31/six-keys-to-excellence-at-anything/#7f4de8422f29

51: Hill, N. (1997, October 1). *Napoleon Hill's Keys to Success: The 17 Principles of Personal Achievement.* TarcherPerigee.

52: Podrazik, J. (2012, December 31). 'Be Responsible for Your Own Life,' Says Oprah. Retrieved from https://www.huffpost.com/entry/be-responsible-take-responsibility-oprah_n_2330820

53: Discipline is the bridge between goals and accomplishment. -Jim Rohn. Retrieved from https://www.pinterest.com/pin/28710516351409016/?lp=true

54: Ladish, L. (2017, July 5). "Keep pushing forward": Three Latino Retail Entrepreneurs Tell Us How They Got There. Retrieved from https://www.nbcnews.com/news/latino/keep-pushing-forward-three-latino-retail-entrepreneurs-share -success-stories-n779701

55: Helen Keller Quotes. Retrieved from https://www.brainyquote.com/quotes/ helen_keller_382259

56: Freeland, G. (2018, June 1). Talent Wins Games, Teamwork Wins Championships. Retrieved from https://www.forbes.com/sites/grantfreeland/2018/06/01/talent-wins -games-teamwork-wins-championships/#7f6f46ea4c8f

57: Vince Lombardi Investoquotia. Retrieved from http://investoquotia.com/ motivators/vince-lombardi/

58: Henry Ford Quotes. Retrieved from https://www.brainyquote.com/quotes/ henry_ford_384400

59: Atlassian. (2019, July 31). A Woman's Place is on the Team. Retrieved from https://www.atlassian.com/blog/inside-atlassian/beyond-hidden-figures-8-women -teams-changed-the-world

60: A Quote by Erastus Wiman. Retrieved from https://www.goodreads.com/ quotes/155452-nothing-is-ever-lost-by-courtesy-it-is-the-cheapest

61: 37 Life-changing Dale Carnegie Quotes From His Two Legendary Books | The Business Quotes. Retrieved from https://www.thebusinessquotes.com/dale -carnegie-quotes/

62: Theodore Roosevelt Quotes. Retrieved from https://www.brainyquote.com/ quotes/theodore_roosevelt_122116

63: The Only Opinion About Your Dream that Really Counts is Yours. Retrieved from https://www.askideas.com/66-all-time-best-others-opinion-quotes-and -sayings/the-only-opinion-about-your-dream-that-really-counts-is-yours-the -negative-comments-of-others-merely-reflect-their-limitations-not-yours-cynthia -kersey-2/

64: A Wise Man Makes His Own Decisions; An Ignorant Man Follows Public Opinion. Retrieved from https://tinybuddha.com/wisdom-quotes/a-wise-man -makes-his-own-decisions-an-ignorant-man-follows-public-opinion/

65: A Quote by Ryan Blair. Retrieved from https://www.goodreads.com/ quotes/7648357-if-it-s-important-you-ll-find-a-way-if-it-s-not

66: Jack Canfield Quotes. Retrieved from https://www.brainyquote.com/quotes/ jack_canfield_637648

67: Brian Tracy Quotes. Retrieved from https://www.brainyquote.com/quotes/ brian_tracy_385850

68: Leo Buscaglia Quotes. Retrieved from https://www.brainyquote.com/quotes/ leo_buscaglia_108583

69: Denis Waitley Quotes. Retrieved from https://www.brainyquote.com/quotes/ denis_waitley_125834

70: Blockbuster Exec Laughed At Marc Randolph Netflix $50 Million Sale Offer. (2019, September 18). Retrieved from https://toofab.com/2019/09/18/blockbuster -exec-laughed-at-netflix-when-they-offered-to-sell-for-50million-in-2000/

71: Srully Blotnick Quote. Retrieved from https://quotefancy.com/quote/1593178/ Srully-Blotnick-What-looks-like-a-loss-may-be-the-very-event-which-is -subsequently

72: Emerson, R.W. (2012, March 15). *The Selected Works of Ralph Waldo Emerson.* Graphic Arts Books.

73: Burrow, M. (2019, July 17). Teaneck Woman Who Saved Home by Baking Apple Cakes Celebrates 10 Years as Entrepreneur. Retrieved from https://northjersey. com/story/news/bergen/teaneck/2019/07/17/teaneck-woman-who-saved-home -baking-apple-cakes-celebrates-10-years/1730436001/

74: Henry Ford Quotes. Retrieved from https://www.brainyquote.com/quotes/ henry_ford_121339

75: Vince Lombardi Quotes. Retrieved from https://www.brainyquote.com/quotes/ vince_lombardi_122285

76: Street, E. (2017, February 15). Overcoming Obstacles: How FDR's Paralysis Made Him a Better President. Retrieved from https://www.learningliftoff.com/overcoming-obstacles-how-fdrs-paralysis-made-him-a-better-president/

77: Mackinnon, L. A. K. (2007, April 19). Quote of The Week – Crawford on Creativity | Think Differently! Retrieved from https://www.think-differently.org/2007/04/quote-of-week-crawford-on-creativity/

78: Dee Hock Quotes. Retrieved from https://www.brainyquote.com/quotes/dee_hock_392459

79: Walt Disney Quotes. Retrieved from https://www.brainyquote.com/quotes/walt_disney_130027

80: Fred Smith. (2008, October 9). Retrieved from https://www.entrepreneur.com/article/197542

81: Hill, N. (2019, March 1). *Think and Grow Rich.* Sound Wisdom LLC.

82: A Quote by Albert Einstein. Retrieved from https://www.goodreads.com/quotes/556030-imagination-is-more-important-than-knowledge-for-knowledge-is-limited

83: Jeff Bezos. (2019, September 5). Retrieved from https://www.biography.com/business-figure/jeff-bezos

84: A Quote by Deepak Chopra. Retrieved from https://www.goodreads.com/quotes/67658-there-are-many-aspects-to-success-material-wealth-is-only

85: Anxiety and Depression Association of America. Physical Activity Reduces Stress | Anxiety and Depression Association of America, ADAA. Retrieved from https://adaa.org/understanding-anxiety/related-illnesses/other-related-conditions/stress/physical-activity-reduces-st

86: Coulson, J., Mckenna, J., & Field, M. (2008). Exercising at work and self-reported work performance. *International Journal of Workplace Health Management*, 1(3), 176–197. doi: 10.1108/17538350810926534

87: Buddha Quotes. Retrieved from http://thinkexist.com/quotation/the_secret_of_health_for_both_mind_and_body_is/147332.html

88: William Penn Quotes. Retrieved from https://www.brainyquote.com/quotes/william_penn_107902

89: Bruni, F. (2018, September 18). The Amputee Who Showed Everyone. Retrieved from https://www.nytimes.com/2018/09/18/opinion/shaquem-griffin-football-amputee.html

90: Johns Hopkins Medicine. The Power of Positive Thinking. Retrieved from https://www.hopkinsmedicine.org/health/wellness-and-prevention/the-power-of-positive-thinking

91: Thomas Carlyle Quotes. Retrieved from https://www.brainyquote.com/quotes/thomas_carlyle_118220

92: Charles Richards Quotes. Retrieved from https://www.goodreads.com/author/quotes/452105.Charles_Richards

93: Walker, J. (2012, July 20). CFI Reports. Retrieved from https://www.fcimag.com/articles/85198-cfi-reports

94: Tracy, B. (2019, October 17). The 80 20 Rule Explained (a.k.a. Pareto Principle) | Brian Tracy. Retrieved from https://www.briantracy.com/blog/personal-success/how-to-use-the-80-20-rule-pareto-principle/

95: Lee Iacocca Quotes. Retrieved from https://www.brainyquote.com/quotes/lee_iacocca_133508

96: Benjamin Franklin Quotes. Retrieved from https://www.brainyquote.com/quotes/benjamin_franklin_141119

97: Dave Ramsey Quote. Retrieved from https://quotefancy.com/quote/1377750/Dave-Ramsey-Those-who-don-t-manage-their-money-will-always-work-for-those-who-do

98: Economy, P. (2019, July 28). 17 Quotes About Money That Will Also Change Your Attitude About Life. Retrieved from https://www.inc.com/peter-economy/17-quotes-about-money-that-will-also-change-your-attitude-about-life.html

99: A Quote by Henry Ford. Retrieved from https://www.goodreads.com/quotes/638-whether-you-think-you-can-or-you-think-you-can-t-you-re

100: Will Durant Quotes. Retrieved from https://www.brainyquote.com/quotes/will_durant_145967

101: Alexander Graham Bell Quotes. Retrieved from https://www.brainyquote.com/quotes/alexander_graham_bell_408695

102: Judith Wright Quotes. Retrieved from https://www.brainyquote.com/quotes/judith_wright_393014

103: Holly Holm Quotes. Retrieved from https://www.brainyquote.com/quotes/holly_holm_739771

104: A Quote by Jorge Cruise. Retrieved from https://www.goodreads.com/quotes/1333690-remember-that-setbacks-are-only-challenges-in-disguise-look-at

105: A Quote by Mark Twain. Retrieved from https://www.goodreads.com/quotes/219455-the-secret-of-getting-ahead-is-getting-started-the-secret

106: A Quote by Ralph Waldo Emerson. Retrieved from https://www.goodreads.com/quotes/137146-patience-and-fortitude-conquer-all-things

Joe Florentine

Joe Florentine has spent 40 years studying the teachings of prominent self-help experts. He received his first copy of *Think & Grow Rich* by Dr. Napoleon Hill as a young adult and used the principles within, among others, to grow his real estate company into a multi-million-dollar business and to find happiness and success in his personal life. After retirement from real estate, he knew he wanted to share the success lessons he's practiced and he founded Success Cornerstone, an organization dedicated to educating young adults and older on ways to live a more successful life. He penned *The Foundation of a Successful Life* to support that very mission.

Erica Florentine

Erica Florentine is a writer whose work has appeared in outlets including Bustle, SparkPeople.com, Thought Catalog, TheRichest.com, HealthU.com, *Fitness* and *Delaware Today* magazines and more. Erica was first exposed to self-help teachings more than a decade ago and has consistently practiced those lessons to excel in her career. With those lessons in place, she's had

the opportunity to work on communications and public relations efforts for international companies including Coca-Cola, Johnson & Johnson, Mondelēz, Nestle and Merck, and most recently joined forces with her father to co-found Success Cornerstone. Learn more about Success Cornerstone by visiting www.SuccessCornerstone.com.